YEARLING BOOKS/YOUNG YEARLINGS/YEARLING CLASSICS are designed especially to entertain and enlighten young people. Patricia Reilly Giff, consultant to this series, received her bachelor's degree from Marymount College and a master's degree in history from St. John's University. She holds a Professional Diploma in Reading and a Doctorate of Humane Letters from Hofstra University. She was a teacher and reading consultant for many years, and is the author of numerous books for young readers.

For a complete listing of all Yearling titles, write to
Dell Readers Service,
P.O. Box 1045,
South Holland, IL 60473.

Advance of American Forces
in southern Okinawa in 1945

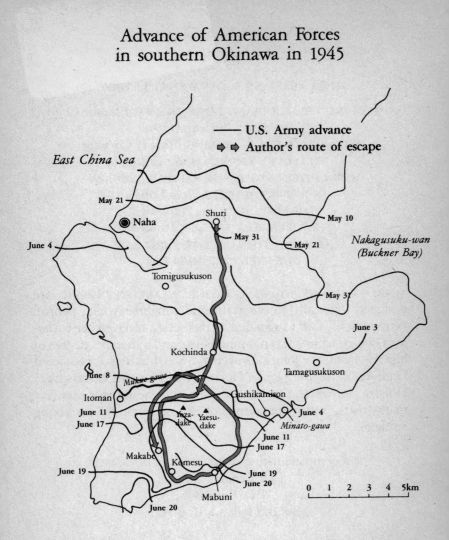

— U.S. Army advance
⇨ ⇨ Author's route of escape

East China Sea

*Nakagusuku-wan
(Buckner Bay)*

May 21

Naha

Shuri

May 10

May 31

May 21

June 4

May 31

Tomigusukuson

June 3

Kochinda

Tamagusukuson

June 8

Mukue-gawa

Itoman

Gushikamison

June 4

June 11

June 17

Yoza-dake

Yaesu-dake

Minato-gawa

June 11

June 17

Makabe

Komesu

June 19

June 19

June 20

Mabuni

0 1 2 3 4 5km

June 20

Source: *Okinawa: The Last Battle* and *Okinawa: Victory in the Pacific* published by the U.S. Army.

THE GIRL WITH THE WHITE FLAG

TOMIKO HIGA
Translated by DOROTHY BRITTON

A Yearling Book

Published by
Dell Publishing
a division of
Bantam Doubleday Dell Publishing Group, Inc.
666 Fifth Avenue
New York, New York 10103

This edition was originally published in Japanese by Kodansha, Ltd., Tokyo International.

Photos courtesy of Tomiko Higa, John Hendrickson, National Archives, Kyodo Tsushin, and Defense Agency Research Center.

ISBN: 0-440-40720-6

Reprinted by arrangement with Kodansha International Ltd.

Printed in the United States of America

November 1992

10 9 8 7 6 5 4 3 2

CWO

Contents

INTRODUCTION

On June 25, 1945, on the war-ravaged island of Okinawa, a young American army signal corps photographer took a remarkable photograph. It showed a little barefoot girl in tattered clothes waving a piece of white cloth tied to a crooked stick. The photograph made an indelible impression on me when I saw it at the time in a magazine. Although it did not become as famous as the scene of planting the Stars and Stripes on Iwo Jima's Mount Suribachi, or the photo years later of the little naked girl fleeing a napalm attack in Vietnam, nevertheless it had the same memorable quality.

The Japanese army in Okinawa was a hundred thousand strong, and it had taken the Americans three months of fierce fighting to overcome such opposition. The extensive death and devastation, including the firebombing of Naha, the island's capital, was in effect a sacrifice to gain time for Japan to assemble forces for a possible last stand on its mainland.

During the battle, a quarter of a million Japanese perished, over half of them civilians. Many of the island's inhabitants, herded together, took their own lives en masse. Considerable numbers died of starvation and disease. Others, suspected of being spies, fell victim to the Japanese army itself.

At last, the Japanese army on Okinawa ceased resistance and hostile activities, succumbing to the all-out offensive by the Americans. On that day in late June, soldiers and civilians, holed up in the multitude of coastal caves in southeastern Okinawa, began coming out to surrender.

Two U.S. Army combat photographers were looking around for interesting picture material. John Hendrickson was taking random still shots and Richard Bagley was taking moving pictures. Their duty was to photograph what was going on and send their film back to Guam for processing and subsequent use by Army Intelligence as well as in public relations.

Surrendering soldiers were being searched for weapons and grenades that they might be hiding in their clothing, after which they were sent to a holding area where they were made to sit in a group on the ground. The two cameramen thought it would be more interesting to photograph the soldiers and civilians as they came out of the caves, so they climbed a hill to higher ground. Suddenly, along came a little girl among the soldiers.

When I saw Hendrickson's photograph in the magazine years ago, I remember thinking how cowardly it was of the Japanese soldiers walking behind her to have sent the young child with her white flag on ahead for protection. Indeed, I believe the caption implied as much. However, Tomiko Higa—who was the little girl in the picture—most emphatically denies this, explaining that she had no connection whatever with the soldiers. She had come along all by herself, quite independently, from an entirely different direction. It just happened that while she walked she had been joined by the soldiers.

John Hendrickson, then only twenty-seven, knew nothing of what had followed his photographic masterpiece until forty-three years had passed and he was living in retirement with his wife Elsie, in Texas City, Texas.

Tomiko Higa had grown up and was happily married. After working for many years in the Okinawa branch of the American Express office, she had embarked on the study of law at the University of Okinawa. She was busy with her studies, and had not yet made her experiences public. It wasn't until she came across John Hendrickson's photograph one day while browsing in an English-language bookstore that her wartime memories came flooding back. Still she remained silent, reluctant to bring up her past. It was only several years later, when movie film footage of her holding the white flag became public and drew conjectures about the little girl, that she felt compelled to identify herself and set some of the facts straight. Ultimately, it was her almost miraculous and emotional meeting with John Hendrickson, ten years after having first discovered the existence of the photograph, that finally gave her an opportunity to resolve the secret torments she had locked deep in her heart. Had it not been for the photograph, this book might never have been written. In it she describes only what she remembers clearly. Where she was not sure of her exact route, or the sequence of events, she has consulted American army records.

Tomiko Higa is humble about the experiences she describes in this book. But if this account of war on Okinawa, as seen through the eyes of a seven-year-old, can serve in some measure to comfort the souls of the old couple who taught her the value of human life, as well as the souls of many, many others who died so tragically, and if it can encourage people to strive harder for world peace so that no child shall ever again have to wander about lost on a battlefield, she feels it will have been worthwhile.

Dorothy Britton
Hayama, Japan
December 1990

Remembering Father's words to die with a brave smile,
the author waves at the camera.

THE PEACEFUL ISLAND
OF OKINAWA

My Home

I was born in Shuri, the ancient capital of Okinawa,
which is now part of the city of Naha. Shuri was the
capital of the Ryukyu kingdom for about 700 years, from
the end of the twelfth century to the end of the nineteenth century. It was a flourishing town, having much
cultural intercourse with China and the countries of
Southeast Asia.

Shurei Gate, which visitors to Okinawa are invariably
shown, was the secondary entrance to Shuri Castle. Its
inscription is said to mean "Nation of Peace." The pre-
sent gate is a replica, the original edifice having been
destroyed by fire during the Pacific War.

I was the last of nine children born to Chokusho and
Kame Matsukawa. The Matsukawa family were heredi-
tary samurai in the service of the Ryukyuan kings. My
father was very proud of this, and brought up his children strictly. Although I was the youngest, there was
never any question of my being spoiled.

Often, when I had been naughty, I would be made to undergo merciless punishments such as having to sit on my legs in the formal posture on the tatami, with my hands tied behind my back, for half a day, or having my bare bottom thrashed till it was scarlet with a long bamboo ruler, or being made to go without lunch or supper.

Ours was a highly respected household, and villagers going by on their way to or from the fields would seldom pass by without stopping to inquire about my father's health.

Our house had a thatched roof and was built in the traditional Okinawan farmhouse style. It faced east, and had a spacious earthen-floored entrance hall beyond which was a wooden-floored area that served as both living and dining room. Next to that was a room about twelve feet square that served as the bedroom for all of us. Unlike most houses in mainland Japan, each room had an outdoor entrance. The ceilings were high and the roof so thickly thatched that even at the height of summer it was cool at night. It was a pleasant house to live in.

The house was built on the northern end of a plot of land about a hundred feet east and west and a hundred and thirty feet north and south. A stream about three feet wide ran behind the main house, and hedges enclosed the property on the front and sides. The hedges were planted with things like the sturdy sea hibiscus, its slender branches covered with yellow flowers, banyan trees from which hung tufts of beard-like aerial roots, and hibiscus bushes with large red flowers. The banyan tree and sea hibiscus make particularly good windbreaks for a place like Okinawa where the wind can be very strong, and are still used around large estates.

Along the hedge stood the livestock sheds in a row, with spaces in between. The goat shed was on the north side of the main house. The horses were stabled in a handsome thatched roof barn with a loft in which things like straw and farm implements were stored. My father often used to lie down for a rest up there in between his chores.

Looking out from the house, you could see the cow shed on the right, and the pigsty to the south, at one side. It was an unusual pigsty. Like old farmhouses in mainland Japan, we had an outside toilet, but unlike the mainland, our toilet was in front of the pigsty. The pigs obligingly consumed the human waste on its way to the adjoining cesspit.

Another unusual feature was that a single large sea hibiscus had been planted right beside the toilet. Its leaves were big and round and could be nicely softened by crumpling in the hand to provide an excellent substitute for toilet paper.

With the neighing of the horses, morning and evening, on one side, and the mooing of the cows on the other, which would start off the goats, followed by the pigs, it was all very animated.

A road just wide enough for two horse-drawn carts to pass ran in front of our house. By the side of the road opposite the house was a well surrounded by a stone wall and shaded by a large fan palm. You could see the reflection of the palm's generous, fan-shaped leaves in the well as they quivered in the breeze, and the well water was so clear you could see right to the bottom. The water always looked so deliciously inviting. It was thought from ancient times that the roots of the fan palm were able to purify water as it seeped through the earth, so these trees were often planted near wells. Also, the leaf of the fan palm could be formed into a receptacle for use in times of drought when there was so little water in the well that a bucket would have stirred up the mud at the bottom. The outer edge of the leaf was bent inwards, bunched together, and tied, and a slender stick about 8 inches long was passed through to the stem end to form a sort of bowl with a handle which was attached to the well-rope. It was then let down gently into the well. Clear water seeped in until the "bowl" was full, and then it was raised carefully to the surface. In a place like Okinawa, where drinking water was scarce, this sort of ingenuity was important.

I led a happy outdoor life at our farm and was as brown as a berry. But one spring, three months before my sixth birthday, came the saddest day of my life. It was the day my mother died. My dear, sweet mother.

The Pacific War, which had begun with the announcement from Imperial Headquarters that "Our Imperial Army and Navy have entered a state of war with the British and American forces in the Western Pacific," had already been under way for two years and three months and the situation was pretty bad, but as yet there was no feeling of tension that the war would reach us in Okinawa.

Just before she died, Mother called me to her bedside and said, "I'll be watching over you, Tomiko, until you're eighteen." She gazed into my eyes very, very steadily, and then her eyes suddenly twitched, and that was the end. She had been suffering from acute meningitis, and the disease had taken a turn for the worse.

I clasped the knees of my dead mother to my tiny bosom. Her knees were thin and bony, and although I was barely six, my arms went easily round them with space to spare. When Mother had been well, her knees had been round and soft and ample and had felt so lovely and downy to sit upon. I could never have got my arms around them then.

My mother, who, rain or shine, be it hot or blowing a gale, never took a single day's rest from caring for us children. My mother—always smiling, always tender. My mother—so in love with my father that the villagers called them the "mandarin duck couple." My mother—dead.

It happened on the nineteenth of March 1944. My two oldest sisters were already married and living somewhere else, and my two oldest brothers were also away, one in China serving in the army and the other working on the mainland. My mother's death was sudden, and conditions in Okinawa at that time made it difficult to get word to them. Even if we had been able to do so, wartime conditions would have prevented them from getting home quickly, so the only members of the family at her bedside were my father, my older sisters Yoshiko and Hatsuko, my older brother Chokuyu and I must the five of us.

As I clutched Mother's knees, which were gradually losing their warmth, I stole a glance at my father's face beside me. My brother and sisters on Mother's other side were also looking at Father. When he realized we were watching him, Father straightened his back and said, "I think your mother was probably fortunate to have been able to die now, with her family around her, because Okinawa may very soon become a battlefield, and when that happens there may be terrible confusion and families may become separated. It was better this way, with us here around her. Better than when it becomes a battlefield. Better." When he had finished speaking, he looked at each of us in turn, my brother, my sisters, and me, and then he made several tiny little nods.

I was only five years and nine months old at the time, and I did not understand what Father meant. Thinking about it now, I think he wanted to let us know how severe wartime conditions in Okinawa were going to become and to prepare us to be strong. And I think he wanted us to realize how important it was for us to have been able to be with our mother when she died, in still peaceful conditions. That is why he used the word "fortunate."

Hugging my mother's knees, I don't know why I thought of it then, but a scene came into my mind of a moonlit night in the garden. My father was playing the samisen (we call it a *sanshin* in Okinawa) and singing:

> *The moon, it changeth not,*
> *This night and yesteryear;*
> *But that which ever changeth*
> *Is man's fickle heart.*

My father was extremely fond of ancient Ryukyuan songs, and he had a good voice. My mother and I were listening spellbound.

When he had finished singing and was sipping his millet brandy, Mother said, fingering her long hair, "Darling, I'd like to cut my hair short."

"No, no! You mustn't do that!" he answered immediately. My father greatly admired Mother's long, lustrous, black hair and took pride in it. Mother looked at Father in speechless astonishment, amazed by his unexpectedly strong reaction.

Father began to play the samisen once more, and I listened enthralled. Then I suddenly glanced at Mother, who was beside me, and noticed that she had fallen asleep. I looked toward Father to let him know, but he seemed to be already aware of the fact, for he was looking at her tenderly as he played. He abruptly stopped playing and said, "Tomiko, we mustn't let your mother catch cold. I'm going to put her to bed, so would you lift up the mosquito net?" "All right," I replied, and went in and lifted up the edge of the net and held it as high as I could, standing on tiptoe. Father lifted Mother up in his big, strong arms, and gently laid her in bed. "She's fast asleep," he whispered, as he brushed aside the hair that had fallen over her brow.

Somehow I couldn't help thinking that Mother was really very anxious to cut her hair, and I wanted to ask Father to please let her do it. I looked up at him, but he must have guessed what was in my mind, for he pre-empted me by saying, "It's time you went to bed, Tomiko." Father's words startled me into action, and I immediately crawled into the mosquito net just as I was. Father was a very strict man, and I never had an opportunity to beg him to let Mother cut her hair and thereby help her to get her wish.

I tried not to wake Mother as I got inside the net and lay down beside her. But to my surprise, Mother, whom I thought was asleep, drew me to her and started to fan me with a fan palm leaf. Its cool breeze gently caressed my face as the fan went flap, flap, and then, gradually, the flaps became fewer and farther between and finally stopped altogether. I nuzzled my face in between my mother's breasts, where their softness enveloped me, and I fell asleep lulled by the rhythm of her heart.

Next morning, I found Mother at the well washing her hair. She seemed to be having trouble drawing up the full bucket, which looked dreadfully heavy. Then Father came and helped her rinse her long hair. After he had rinsed it over and over again, he took a comb and combed it for her. It was typical of their great love for each other.

But Mother did not seem as well as usual, and when

she saw me she only managed a weak smile. That was strange, for her smiles were normally like sunshine itself. Looking back, I think she must have already been ailing.

Very soon after Mother's death, Father himself cut my hair off short like a boy's. To this day I do not know why he did it. He was always saying, "Tomiko has inherited her mother's hair. It's so black," so it may be that my hair reminded him of my mother and made him sad. Or it may have been that he sensed how soon the war would be upon us and felt that I would have an easier time if I looked like a boy. I was not unhappy at having my hair cut. It made me feel light and carefree, and I thought how Mother would have liked feeling that way, too, and I was just the tiniest bit sorry for her.

My Father

My father, being the Matsukawas' third son, set up a household of his own on the outskirts of Shuri and farmed. Father was a very hard worker, and had many talents. He was particularly good at writing with a brush. In those days schoolchildren were required to have a patch of cloth sewn onto the left breast of whatever they were wearing, on which was written their name, address, blood group, etc., and my sister once told me that on seeing hers, which had been inscribed by our father, her teacher was extremely impressed by the superb calligraphy. Word must have got around, for villagers often came to ask him to inscribe things for them. He was always happy to oblige, and would start rubbing his

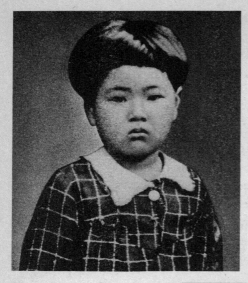

The author at five years of age. Her once long hair was cut short by her father soon after her mother's death.

The author's father was a source of wisdom for her.

inkstick on his inkstone immediately. I would sit down beside him and watch fascinated as his brush slid over the white paper and the beautiful characters emerged.

"You must make the ink with great care. You mustn't do it haphazardly, or be in a hurry," my father would say to me as he slowly rubbed the inkstick. Soon the room would be filled with the faint fragrance of Indian ink and an indescribable atmosphere of elegant solemnity.

My father was also good at figures and accounts. There is a financing scheme in Okinawa called *moai* in which villagers each contribute money to a fund from which money can be loaned to those in need, priority being given to whoever can pay the most interest. My father was in charge of the accounts. It was a very important function, so at banquets following village events, sake was always poured out first for Father, who would be all smiles.

Another of Father's skills was weaving bamboo baskets. Spreading a straw mat on the ground in the garden, he would sit down and start splitting bamboo stalks he had cut from the grove into fine strips, which he used to make all sorts of baskets for various purposes, such as those for hanging up local doughnuts, large-mesh ones for penning ducks, and baskets for washing sweet potatoes. In Father's nimble fingers, the fine strips of bamboo danced about as if they were alive, and in no time he would turn them into a basket, as if by magic.

Once, when Father sent me to the bamboo grove behind the house to cut him a bamboo stalk, I stepped on a bamboo stump, sharp as an arrowhead, that pierced my foot clear through to my instep. Blood gushed out as I frantically withdrew my foot, but I kept from crying, since the accident had happened through my own carelessness. Somehow, I managed to endure the pain and get back to the house. When he saw the blood, Father was naturally alarmed, and stopped work and carried me inside, where he attended to my wound.

Father was a person who hardly ever resorted to medicine. In this case, he merely made some Indian ink and poured that into my wound, covered the open ends with calligraphy paper, and bandaged my foot. It was rough-and-ready treatment, but some days later when he undid the bandage, the wound had completely healed; only the black stain of the Indian ink remained on my sole and instep. The scars are clearly visible to this day.

Speaking of rough-and-ready remedies, there was the time I had a boil on my thigh. It was so painful and swollen that I said, "Father, when do you think this boil will heal?" After feeling it, he replied, "It's not ripe yet. You'll have to wait a bit." He ignored it for days. There was no question, of course, of his taking me to a hospital. As the boil grew redder and more swollen, however, I could not help worrying about it in my childish way.

Then, one day, he called me over to the stove. "Tomiko, we're going to destroy that boil today," he said, thrusting a poker into the fire. When the point was red hot he took it out, and holding my thigh with his other hand, he pierced the boil. It was all done so quickly that I had no time to say it hurt or to cry. All I remember is that the pus shot out onto Father's face.

"And now, grit your teeth, Tomiko," he said, "because I'm going to squeeze out all the pus." Before I knew what was happening, he had started to squeeze the boil with his big, strong hands. When blood appeared, he took a plantain leaf, heated it over the fire, stuck it over the wound, and the treatment was over.

"Well, that's that. You were a brave girl," he said, gently stroking my head.

Thinking about it now, his treatment seems rather drastic, but a few days later the boil had healed. My father was certainly a man with remarkable skills and his own way of doing things.

But he had one very awkward habit. It always happened when he was in a jolly mood after having had too much to drink.

"You poor things," he would say, "you must be fed up with being in the same place all the time. I'm going to let you out." And he would open the pens and let out the horse first, and then the cows, and then the goats, and then the chickens, and finally the pigs.

It was terrible. The whole grounds would be filled with animals. It was like an animals' pedestrian mall. The cows and horses even came right into the house, acting as if they owned the place. And my father would watch them, beaming with satisfaction.

"My! Aren't you enjoying yourselves!" he would say, patting them, while my brother and I were so terrified we didn't even dare get into our futons at night for fear we might be trampled, and had to take refuge in the barn loft.

After that came the task of collecting the animals. It was far too big a job for just my father, sister, and brother, and the villagers had to help out. It didn't take too long to round up most of the animals, including the cows, but the horses could gallop so fast that they would disappear into the distance, and sometimes it was days before they were found. On those occasions my father's eyes would look hollow with fatigue.

Once when Father got drunk and let the animals out, he went off as usual to find one of the horses, and by nightfall he still hadn't returned. He was quite indifferent to our worrying, and it was almost daybreak by the time he came back with the horse. He was lying stretched out across its back like a dead man. It wasn't Father that had brought the horse home, it was the horse, all on its own, that had brought Father back to the house. Okinawan sake has a high alcohol content, and when we got Father down off the horse, his breath was still very pungent.

There is a tradition in Okinawa at busy times like harvest for farmers to help each other out gratis. Once, on our way home all together, after having given such help, Father was carrying me piggyback, which I was enjoying very much. Then either my brother or my sister said, "You must be tired, Daddy. Why don't you make Tomiko walk?" They came over and peered at me, and I knew that if they thought I was awake they would make me get down. My eyes were already closed, but I shut them even tighter, and clung to my father's broad back like a tiny frog. My father's back was lovely and warm, and over his shoulder I could see the moon shining beautifully bright and softly illuminating everything all around. I wished the way home would go on forever. I can still remember the warmth of my father's back today, over forty years later.

Chokuyu started going to school the year I was six, which meant that now, when Father went off to his fields, I was left all alone in the house. I did not mind that, but I had to make Father's lunch. About all I was capable of preparing was fried vegetables and boiled potatoes, which I would put in his lunch box together with some rice.

Placing Father's lunch box in one basket and mine in another, and hanging them from each end of a carrying pole, which I balanced on my shoulders, I would hurry along the path through the hills that led to the field where my father was, after making sure that the sun was directly above my head. (Father taught me this was the way I could tell the time. Besides, except for Father's wristwatch, which he kept carefully put away, there was no clock in the house.) I took the carrying pole because of the danger of stray dogs and because it was scary on that hill path, with pampas grass taller than I was growing thickly on either side, out of which turtledoves would suddenly fly up with a great beating of wings. It was a wonderful relief when I finally reached the field and caught sight of my father. My high spirits would be restored, and when he heard me call out to him, he would stop work and come out onto the path to meet me. Then he would sit down in a corner of the field and start eating the lunch I had made, with obvious enjoyment.

"You've certainly learned how to cook rice well, Tomiko" he would say, smiling. But much as I liked making Father's lunch, I wished to myself that Father had time to play with me more.

One day, Father said, "Tomiko, I won't need any lunch today, because you're coming to the field with me."

So he was going to play with me, I thought, and feeling very sure about it, I skipped along as I followed him to the field. But mine was a hasty conclusion. He wanted me to clear the vines where he was going to dig potatoes.

"You can cut them with this," he said, handing me a scythe. The large scythe was so heavy for my tiny hands to hold, that I was not able to cut very fast. But father didn't seem to take any notice, and I went on cutting, drenched in sweat and out of breath, my palms red and sore.

Then I suddenly looked up, and seeing that the sun was directly overhead, I said,

"Daddy, it's noon. Who's going to bring us our lunch?"

"Nobody," he replied.

I began to worry about what we were going to do about lunch. But I kept quiet. Then Father said, putting his arm around my shoulder, "Food isn't just what you roast or boil, you know. You can eat giant radishes and carrots and tomatoes, and even sweet potatoes, raw.

There, pull yourself up a radish and a carrot and pick yourself a tomato. Go and wash them in the stream over there, and eat them."

After showing me how to avail myself of the vegetables he led me to a nearby stream, showing me on the way a herb called *nigana*, which he picked and ate. I tried some too, but it was so bitter it made my mouth pucker, and I spit it out right away. The radish, carrot and sweet potato were delicious by comparison. I would never have thought you could eat sweet potatoes raw. From then on I began to look forward to the next time I would not be required to cook a picnic lunch.

That day came sooner than I expected. And, moreover, I was not even required to accompany Father to the field. After he had set off, I swept up the fallen leaves in the garden and was burning them, when I had a marvelous idea. I had discovered several handfuls of soybeans in a corner in the house, and thought how good they would taste roasted in the embers of the bonfire. Father had said there were all sorts of things you could add to your picnic lunch besides rice. Yes! Why not! I got an empty can from the kitchen, put in a handful of beans, and set it among the embers. Pretty soon, the whole garden began to be filled with the fragrant aroma of roasting beans. They're just about done, I thought, and taking the can out of the ashes, I tried a couple. They were delicious! Crunching ecstatically, I finished them all, and put the empty can back where I had found it.

When Father returned in the afternoon he noticed the

fragrant aroma of the beans and said, "Tomiko, you roasted the beans and ate them, didn't you?"

"Yes, I did" I replied, proudly, as much as to say, "Don't you think I did rather well?" But Father's reaction was quite the opposite to what I expected. Instead of his usual gentle expression, he was livid.

"Those were seed beans I was keeping carefully to plant next year. If you roast them and eat them, how can we plant any next year? You may be a child, but there are things you may do and things you may not. Come here, Tomiko. I'm going to punish you."

He held me under his arm while he bound my hands and feet with rope and put me in a net bag which he suspended from a sea hibiscus branch over the cesspit. Leaving me there, he went back to his field. The bag I was in was made of coarse rope mesh and was used in those days for carrying things like loads of earth or fertilizer. A man working on a construction site or farm would carry two of them, one suspended at each end of a shoulder pole. I was shocked and terrified.

If I moved even a little, the sea hibiscus branch rocked and swayed, and worse still, creaked as if it might break off. If it broke, I knew I would plop straight down into the cesspit. There was nothing to do but to keep very still. When I had to urinate, it dropped down into the cesspit and caused a horrible smell to rise. Hanging there, it dawned on me finally that I must have done something very bad. Those soybeans had tasted so good, but how bitter they seemed now in retrospect.

My father came home earlier than usual and took me

down from the sea hibiscus branch, and untied me. The rope left purple marks on my hands and feet. Massaging them with his large hands, he said, "It must have hurt. But you've got to learn that seeds are next in importance to life. If you eat them up, you won't have any beans next year. And not only you, but Yoshiko and Hatsuko and Chokuyu. None of you will have any beans to eat. Do you understand? You mustn't ever eat seeds again."

"I'm sorry," I said, and began to cry for the first time.

Presently, Hatsuko and Chokuyu came home from school. Hatsuko was seven years older than I and I called her Nene, short for *O-nesama*, which means "honorable older sister." Chokuyu was three years older than I, and I called him Nini, short for *O-nisama*, "honorable older brother." The three of us were very close, and told each other everything. But I determined that what had happened to me that day would remain a secret between my father and me. I was afraid that if either of them discovered the purple marks on my hands and feet I might start crying again. But fortunately they never noticed.

My father may have had that sort of strict side to him, but after my mother died, he would steal out more and more often into the garden alone at night and stand gazing up at the moon. He used to look so lonely. Seeing that tender side of him made me resolve not to do anything again to upset him.

Nini and I were playmates. There was a girl in the neighborhood only a year older than I, but I do not remember ever playing with her. Nini was much more fun, for he was a genius at thinking up ways to play.

Every day he would take me with him into the hills and fields and invent things to do that I never would have dreamed of: we would put two of the narrow sword-like leaves of the screw pine together and make pinwheels; we would take the metal bands from a discarded barrel and roll them along like hoops; we would go to a small hill called Pengadake and climb its trees and slide down its slopes on a "slide" we made by pressing down clumps of the pampas grass that grew there. Nini had a knack for making things to play with that he found on the spot.

We often played hide and seek and tag by the "turtle-shell" tomb near our house. These family tombs are built in a style peculiar to Okinawa. They are about five-and-a-half yards wide and four-and-a-half yards deep, and are dug into the earth and lined with stone with a very solid round roof shaped like a turtle's shell. There is a small entrance at the front, and inside they are quite roomy, with shelves for holding rows of urns in chronological order, containing the ashes of generations of deceased family members.

Whatever Nini did, I always wanted to do it too and compete with him, but I was no match for fun-loving Nini. I particularly liked climbing trees. When you climbed a tree you could see way down the road as it

Little sister and brother often played at such a tomb, constructed in a "turtle-shell" style peculiar to Okinawa.

wound through the hills. In this way I would watch Mother go off to the market and would stay in the tree for hours until I could see her coming back.

Speaking of tree-climbing, there was a mandarin orange tree growing deep inside a bamboo grove near our house that was laden with fruit in the autumn. You could be sure that fun-loving Nini would hardly ignore the fact. "My! Don't they look good," he said one day, smacking his lips, as he started to creep through the bamboo grove.

"Those oranges belong to someone," I said, tugging at his shirt. "You'd be stealing."

"Yes, I know," Nini replied, "but the owner lives a long way away." He crept through the bamboos and scrambled up the orange tree. I followed him to the base of the tree.

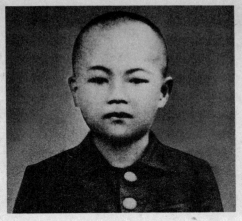

Nini, the author's brother, at eight years of age.

"Nini, why don't you just shake the tree so the oranges fall down?"

"Can't do that. There's a watch dog. If it hears a noise it'll come bounding out. So be quiet."

But just then I began coughing and couldn't stop. I hadn't quite recovered from a bout of whooping cough. The dog heard me and started barking ferociously.

"Oh, gosh! Come on, Tomiko."

Nini slid down the tree, grabbed hold of my hand, and we tore out of the bamboo grove and ran home as fast as our legs would carry us, without looking back. Even now it gives me cold shivers whenever I think of it. Nini never suggested going after those mandarin oranges again.

Once when Nini and I went to the stream for a swim, I suddenly felt something slimy against my body.

"Nini! A snake! Help!" I cried, thinking it might be a poisonous *habu*.

"Don't move, stay right where you are," shouted Nini, quickly coming to my rescue.

Then, after staring into the water for some time, he said, "Silly girl! It was only an eel! You hardly ever find snakes in rivers."

"An eel? But it was slimy and long."

"If it was slimy, it was bound to be an eel. Snakes aren't slimy."

"Oh yeah? Well you sure acted worried. You looked so funny," I said, laughing. Forgetting that he had done it to rescue me, I thought about the agitated way he had leaped into the water, and I laughed until I cried.

"Daddy, we saw an eel in the stream," reported Nini when we reached home.

"Really? Then I'll teach you a way to catch them."

Picking up a bucket, he led Nini and me to the stream. Watch me, Chokuyu," he said, wading in, "first you make a circle with your thumb and middle finger like this, and entice the eel through it. Got it?" While explaining to us, he crouched down and passed his hands through the water a couple of times.

"Got him!"

Straightening himself, he held up his arm for us to see as we stood on the bank. He was gripping a long, fat, writhing eel.

"I want to try," said Nini, jumping into the stream with a splash.

"Me too!" I said, following him. We splashed about,

getting covered in mud from head to foot.

"You won't catch any eels that way," laughed Father. "This is how you do it."

He felt on the bottom and in the twinkling of an eye he brought up his hand tightly gripping an eel. Then, just for the fun of it, he went on catching eel after eel. But Nini and I couldn't catch any at all.

Father beamed with pleasure as he carried home his bucket full of eels. Only one of them, which we had managed to shoo up onto the bank, was ours, but in two or three days, Nini improved his skill so much that although he was not quite up to Father's standard, he was able to bring back a bucket with at least the bottom covered in eels.

Nini was a wonderful playmate for me, and taught me so much.

The Kind and Gentle Soldier

One day, towards the end of March 1945, a year after my mother's death, Father came home in great agitation from delivering foodstuffs to the Signal Corps unit stationed near our house. Father was normally calm and composed and hardly ever got upset, so I thought something terrible must have happened. He called us all together—Yoshiko, Hatsuko, Chokuyu, and me.

"Now I want you all to listen carefully. There's going to be fighting here in Okinawa very soon. Life's not going to be peaceful for us any more. You must be prepared, so that when the time comes you'll be able to

The hill where the Signal Corps unit was once stationed, viewed from the author's former home. This place is now a cemetery.

keep your head and know what to do."

My sisters and brother looked at one another, and I looked at their faces and at my father's face in turn, for I had no way of knowing how to react on my own. It was not until about a month later that I was to learn something of the tragedy of war.

My father at that time was responsible for providing food to the Signal Corps unit and that was how he heard reports on how the war was progressing.

He often told us we must eat the small sweet potatoes because the large ones were for the soldiers. In return, he occasionally brought home cans of sake and sweets they had given him. Sometimes, when Father was busy and couldn't go to the Signal Corps unit himself, Nini and I would take them their freshly-steamed sweet potatoes. They would thank us heartily, and give us sweets, after which they might show us around parts of the Unit, such as their air-raid shelter.

One day, I was watching Nene steam sweet potatoes in the kitchen when I heard a loud splash in the direction of the cesspit. "Nene," I said, "something's fallen into the cesspit."

"Maybe it's a dog," she replied, not taking much interest.

But it sounded too big for a dog, so I ran out to see. It was a soldier, and Father and Nini were pulling him out. I don't know how he happened to fall in, and I knew it was terribly rude of me, but it struck me so funny to see a soldier—usually so spick and span in their uniforms—all covered in smelly muck, that I just couldn't help laughing. Father took him to the well and washed him off and loaned him a suit to put on in place of his soiled uniform.

The soldier and I soon became good friends. He often gave me piggyback rides in the hills, where he would tell me about the place he came from, his family, and especially about his mother. He was very fond of children.

Then after a while, he disappeared, and we didn't see him any more. "I wonder what's happened to that soldier," I used to think, hoping every day that he would come again. But days went by and he never came. Then I had an idea. If I took over some sweet potatoes I would probably see him. So I filled a basket with steamed sweet potatoes and took them to the Signal Corps. But I saw no sign of my soldier anywhere. The other soldiers ate the sweet potatoes and told me how good they were. But as I walked home, swinging the empty basket, I was so disconsolate about not seeing my soldier friend that I couldn't keep the tears from rolling down my cheeks. When I reached home I wanted to ask Father what had happened to the soldier, but for some reason I thought I ought not to ask, so I refrained.

Then one evening, a few days later, I came across a group of soldiers sitting in a circle around a fire in the middle of a field half way between the Signal Corps and our house. Strangely, while there were at least ten soldiers there, I didn't hear any voices. Wondering what they were burning, I went straight up to one of them and asked him.

"We're cremating someone," he replied.

I was dumbfounded. Looking into the flames, I was able to make out a pair of army boots at one end and at the other, where the head would be, I could see an army cap. On impulse, I knelt down with the others. Among the soldiers I happened to recognize one that sometimes came to our house to take delivery of the sweet potatoes. I made up my mind to ask him about "my" soldier.

"That soldier? That's 'im in there among the flames."

I was at a loss for words. I sat in a daze, staring at the fire. That nice, kind soldier, who used to carry me piggyback, lay there in the flames, getting smaller and smaller. In the end, he just turned into ashes.

After the fire had died down, the soldiers picked the bones out of the embers and put them in a small pot and reverently carried it away with them. I had never seen stern soldiers looking so forlorn. I secretly wrapped the remaining ashes in a coltsfoot leaf and buried them beside the stream behind the house. Folding my hands in prayer, I said in my heart, "Dear soldier, this is the best I can do. I hope you don't mind."

He loved the stream. Whenever he came to our house, he never failed to come and stand by the stream, for it reminded him of his faraway home, and his mother. "How I wish I could see my mother," he would say, as he quietly watched the sun go down. "Oh, if I could only hear her voice!" And in spite of the fact that I was standing there by his side, his eyes would fill with tears.

At such times, I would try and cheer him up by finding him a crab. But he would say, "Tomiko, let's put the poor creature back in the stream." And he would let it go.

My soldier sleeps there still, beside the stream. And he lives on in my heart, forever young, and gentle, and kind.

JOINING THE REFUGEES

Waiting for Father

The American soldiers finally landed on Okinawa on the morning of April 1, 1945. Subsequent records show that a fleet of about thirteen hundred ships assembled off Yomitan and Kadena facing the East China Sea on the southwestern coast of the main island of Okinawa and carried out a two-and-a-half hour sea and air bombardment. At the same time, some 60,000 troops proceeded to come ashore from early morning until late afternoon.

Naturally, at the time I was not aware of the military situation. But the anniversary of my mother's death was no sooner over than air raid sirens began to sound from time to time and I would see American war planes in the sky. There was a continuous sound like far-off thunder coming from the area north of Shuri, accompanied by rumblings and thuds that I could feel in the pit of my stomach. I think now that it must have been the April first bombardment. The war had finally come to Okinawa, just as my father had feared.

About a month later, bombs and shells began to fall around our house, and it got so that whenever the siren went we had to take cover in the air-raid shelter my father had dug. The shelter was made of such soft earth that I was afraid it would easily cave in.

"What's the use of a shelter like this?" I asked Father.

"None of the shelters around here can survive if they receive a direct hit," he explained, "but because the earth is so soft there's a chance that the bombs and shells that land nearby may bore into the earth and not explode."

Sure enough, one morning after an air raid, when a man from the village came out of his shelter to urinate, his urine washed the earth away from a gold-colored cylindrical object, which turned out to be an unexploded shell. Just as my father had said, the soft earth had prevented it from going off.

Every day the air raids and the shelling came closer and grew more violent. By the beginning of April 1945, there were hardly any more sweet potatoes left for us to give to the soldiers in the Signal Corps. Almost all the agricultural produce of the village had been put at the disposal of the Army.

Father had to leave the four of us from time to time to go to Makabe, south of where we lived, to collect farm animals that he had pastured there and to see if he could find any produce. Besides farming, he was also personally responsible for providing the Signal Corps stationed near us with food. Because of that work, the Signal Corps Commander managed to get him excused from joining the Civilian Defense Force, so whatever happened, he had to obtain food for the Corps. And it was that which determined the fate of Father and of us four children.

We had no calendars in the house so I do not know the exact date, but I think it must have been around the tenth of April. Just before leaving the house, Father called the four of us together and said, "If by any chance there is an enemy attack in this immediate area while I am away and I can't get back, you will each have to decide for yourselves what to do. But Yoshiko, since you are the oldest, you must look after your sisters and your brother. And the rest of you must do as she says, for she will be taking my place." It seemed to me that

Father was speaking more seriously than he had ever done before. Perhaps he already sensed that the worst was about to happen and wanted us to be prepared. As it happened, those were the last words he ever spoke to us.

That day, the American forces, which had already landed, began their assault on Shuri, where we lived. The noise of the bursting shells seemed thunderously close—far louder and nearer than ever. But we never dreamed that we would not see our father again. We waited for him that night, all the next day and the next. On the third morning, Yoshiko went to the Signals Corps Unit to find out if Father was safe, but far from obtaining any news of him, she was told:

"Fierce fighting is going on all over Shuri. You must escape towards the south as quickly as you can."

Yoshiko was 17, Hatsuko was 13, Chokuyu was 9, and I was nearly 7.

A Glimpse of Hell

When she returned from the Signals Corps Unit, Yoshiko called us together and said, "Father said that if he didn't come back we were to decide for ourselves what to do. I think we must do as he said. So I'm going to take you with me towards the south. Chokuyu and Tomiko, you'd better put some clothes and things together. Hatsuko and I will carry as much as we can. We'd better hurry."

We got ready as soon as we could and left behind us the house we had known so well. Yoshiko looked back at it time and time again. Each time she did, the rest of us did so too. The yellow and red hibiscus blossoms in the hedge looked so pretty. We could see the thatched roofs of the main house and the stable through the branches of the banyan tree.

"I wonder how the ducks are," I said casually.

"Stop talking and walk faster," said Yoshiko crossly, unlike her usual gentle manner.

My two sisters, carrying our bundles on their heads, took the lead as we walked towards the south, and my brother followed behind, holding my hand. We could only walk at night, for in the daytime, the enemy land and air offensive was so heavy that we had to take cover in air-raid shelters and caves. Even at night we did not walk very far before flares would begin to make everything as light as day, followed by explosive shells. It was eerie and terrible, and thinking about it even now makes cold shivers go down my spine.

When we left home, the bundles my sisters carried were so heavy it made their heads ache, but in a few days, only one bundle was left, which Yoshiko managed to carry easily herself. This was because the bundles mostly consisted of food, and we now had only enough rice left for one meal. Yoshiko had asked the people at a tiled house we had passed to let us cook our rice there, but when we also requested permission to spend the night at their house, they were so full up with refugees already that they refused, and we slept, instead, in a nearby cave we found.

Okinawa has many natural caves in the hillsides and

cliffs and along the rocky shore, and you can still find bits of broken dishes and tattered remnants of things left behind by the refugees. Some of the caves still contain human bones.

When Yoshiko returned to the cave with the cooked rice, she found me fast asleep, and although she and the others shook me awake, I kept falling asleep as they tried to get me to eat my meal.

"Tomiko, since it's whole grain rice, chew well or you'll get a stomachache. We've got to start walking again tomorrow, so if you don't eat you'll collapse."

Yoshiko finally slapped my cheek in desperation. I was so surprised by the pain in my cheek and the cross tone of Yoshiko's voice that I opened my eyes to see both my sisters bending over me with concern.

"What is it?" I asked sleepily.

One of the many natural caves in the hillsides and cliffs of southern Okinawa.

"We're worried about you. We were afraid you might be sick."

I noticed that my sisters didn't look as if they had eaten any of the rice. I realized they were saving it for me. I managed to wake myself up and begin eating when there was a deafening explosion—by far the most terrifying noise I had ever heard. It was an enemy shell exploding at extremely close quarters.

I was quite sure we had been hit. But looking at our hands and feet and bodies, they seemed intact. None of the other people in the cave were hurt either. I don't remember how long it was after that, but when things finally quieted down, Hatsuko decided to go out in search of some drinking water.

She did not come back for some time, and Yoshiko became very anxious and restless, pacing in and out of the cave. When Hatsuko finally got back, Yoshiko reproved her tearfully.

"Hat-chan, why did you have to go so far away to get water? I was terribly worried. Please don't go off again and leave us. Let me go instead."

Handing Yoshiko the container she had been clasping to her bosom, Hatsuko said, "You remember the house with the tiled roof where they let us boil our rice? It was blown to bits by that bomb. I started to draw some water from the well there, but there were dead bodies floating in it. It was a long way before I finally found some stagnant water in a field."

"You poor thing," said Yoshiko, over and over again, squeezing her hand.

We couldn't drink the water right away. We had to wait until the dirt and mud had sunk to the bottom. The container was only half full, for Hatsuko had been so shaken by the sight of the demolished house that her hands couldn't stop trembling.

Yoshiko gave me the water to drink first, saying, "Don't shake it and stir up the mud."

I thought Hatsuko should have had the first drink, but she joined Yoshiko in urging me to start, so I took one or two sips. It tasted wonderful.

In 1987, when I began writing this book, I wondered where all that took place, and asked Yoshiko. But she consistently refused to talk about it. So I finally said, "I remember the time you slapped my face and made me eat the last of the rice you had brought from home and cooked. You know, you never told me that you had saved my life. I've always admired you for that."

As I looked steadily at her, she suddenly blurted out, "It was at Makabe."

It was the answer to the questions I had wondered about for so long—why my sisters had wanted to stay at the house with the tiled roof, and why we had remained in that cave for so many days. Makabe was where the people at the Signal Corps unit had told Yoshiko that Father had gone to collect livestock. My sisters believed that if we went there we would have a chance of finding him.

We spent quite a few days in Makabe. During that time, my sisters frequently left Nini and me in the cave and went searching for Father. But far from finding him, they didn't succeed even in finding clues to his whereabouts. In the meantime, the fighting was getting closer, and so we started walking south again, this time without any objective, and simply as refugees, stumbling over bodies in the dark, not knowing whether they were alive or dead.

One horrible scene remains indelibly etched on my brain and still gives me nightmares. It happened a day or two after we left Makabe. A woman was lying on the ground, hit by shrapnel from a bomb, with blood streaming from her chest, and at her breast an infant about a year old lay sucking up the blood. The sight rooted me to the spot. When the baby saw us it lifted its face, whose features were just a mass of blood, and stretched out its arms towards us as if to say, "Carry me!" Its arms, too, were covered with its mother's blood. But we four children were so intent on getting away that there was nothing we could do. There was nothing anyone could do, for masses of wounded were lying all over the place, many of them covered in blood and crying for help.

It was a scene straight out of hell. There is no other way to describe it. And sad and painful though it was, we could not afford to linger, and so we set off again trekking south.

Parting with Nini

I don't know how far we had walked, but we continued on, encouraging one another as we became more and more tired, until finally we saw a long, low hill ahead of us. "Let's spend the night on that hill," said Yoshiko.

Climbing on our hands and knees through a thicket we came to a rather flat area we thought would do, when suddenly we heard a bomb explode above us and someone rolled down the hill enveloped in flames. He had been hit by an incendiary bomb.

Seeing that, Yoshiko decided we had better leave the hill and go down to the shore.

"Tomiko, we must dig a hole to sleep in. Hurry," said Chokuyu, already starting to dig in the sand with his hands. Following his example I started digging right next to him. We managed to make a hole—or rather a hollow—just big enough to hold Nini's and my bottoms. The hollow was too small and shallow to lie down in, so we just sat close together, with our legs stretched out in front and our backs against the side of the hollow. I went to sleep with my head on Nini's shoulder. Nini put his arm around my shoulder and covered us with a piece of cloth. Our sisters slept in a hollow they had dug right beside ours. All the while, shells and machine gun bullets continued to fall about us, near and far, without any let-up. If we had worried about them we would not have been able to sleep at all. We had already resigned ourselves to the horror of the enemy attack.

It did not seem to me that we had slept for more than a few moments when five or six soldiers appeared and shouted in loud voices, "Move off, move off! There's going to be fighting here soon. Go somewhere else!"

I hurriedly tried to shake Nini awake, but he did not

respond. He's fast asleep, I thought, and saw that he was sleeping with his eyes wide open. "Nene!" I called to Hatsuko, "Nini's asleep with his eyes open!" at which Yoshiko hurried over and called his name, "Chokuyu! Chokuyu!"

But Nini just sat there with his eyes wide open.

Yoshiko removed the cloth he had over his head and saw that his head had a hole in it and there was blood all over the back of his head and on his shoulders and down his back. The three of us did not speak for some time. We just sat in a daze surrounding Nini. Finally, each of my two sisters in turn hugged Nini and wept. I couldn't believe Nini was dead, and I couldn't understand why they were crying. "Nini's just asleep," I said, "with his eyes open." And besides, his body had felt warm against mine when I woke. It was explained to me later that a stray bullet had gone through Nini's head and that he probably died instantly. My head and Nini's head could not have been more than eight inches apart at the time. To think that I should have been saved and Nini killed. How cruel fate is.

Yoshiko stared at me for some time. "Tomiko! *You're* all right, aren't you? Aren't you?" She made me stand up then, and felt me all over. When she had satisfied herself that I was not hurt, she hugged me so tightly I could hardly breathe, and her tears kept running down my cheek. I remember how warm her tears were.

My sisters made me sit in the hole they had dug for themselves while they gently laid Nini down in the hollow he and I had occupied and started covering him with sand. When they had covered all but his head I ran over and tried to close his eyes for him. I now understood that he was dead, and I knew he wouldn't be able to sleep properly with his eyes open. But I couldn't make myself do it, because his cheeks were still warm. Yoshiko closed them for him instead.

"Goodbye, Nini" I said, as his eyes were closed, and folded my hands together in prayer, while Hatsuko threw herself down on Nini's body and cried.

In a while, his face disappeared from view, and instead of Nini there was just a little mound of sand, slightly bigger than he. That was the end of his burial.

With her eyes full of tears, Yoshiko clasped both my hands and said, "Tomiko, you're still a little girl and you've got a pretty good chance of living a long time. So if Hatsuko and I don't make it, you must come back for Chokuyu's remains and put them properly in our family tomb. We had to bury him here temporarily because of the war. You'll do it, won't you, Tomiko?" And she went on, "You must remember where this is. It's called Komesu. Komesu. Have you got it? You must remember. Komesu."

She repeated the name over and over again, and although I did not know the characters for it then, I never forgot the name Komesu.

How fortunate Chokuyu was, I thought at the time, to have died there in that hole, and to have had his sisters cover him so lovingly with sand, and I promised Nini faithfully in my heart that I would come back and fetch him one day.

We could not linger there any longer. The soldiers, who had pretended to ignore us while we buried our brother, now came over and told us to move on.

Fleeing Alone

Leaving our hearts there, we walked away from Komesu beach, casting many a backward glance at the mound of sand where we had buried Nini. Komesu, which I later located on the map, is at the southernmost tip of the main island of Okinawa. In our flight, we had covered about nine miles in a direct line from home.

As far as Komesu, Nini had held my hand the whole way, and now I clutched a corner of Hatsuko's garment as I walked. The road was crowded with people who had been driven away from Komesu beach, and I hung on to Hatsuko's clothes very tightly, almost running to

Komesu beach, where Nini lost his life. Many are said to have been temporarily buried here.

keep up, for fear of becoming separated from my sisters.

Some time later, I happened to look up at Hatsuko, whose face was only barely visible in the starlight. To my horror, the face was not Hatsuko's. Nor was it Yoshiko's. It was that of a woman I had never seen before. The woman whose garment I had been clutching all this time was a total stranger. I did not know how it could have happened.

I let go my hand and started running hither and yon, looking at the face of this young woman and that, but could find neither Hatsuko nor Yoshiko anywhere.

I was all alone.

Thinking I would find them soon, I spent the night in a grassy spot away from the road, for sleep had overcome my determination to find my sisters.

Searching for them was impossible in the daytime, however, as enemy action was so severe that all one could do was hide in a cave until nightfall. Moreover, I had nothing with me at all—nothing to eat and no change of clothes—and I felt terribly lonely and frightened.

I could not wait for night to fall, and left my place of hiding. I ran from cave to cave calling out "Sister! Sister!" only to be shooed away by the cave's denizens the way you would shoo away an unwanted cat or dog.

Finally, exhausted, I found a little cave in the rocks by the shore where nobody was, and fell asleep from sheer relief. But I awoke before dawn, feeling very cold, to find waves washing over me and reaching up to my head. It must have been low tide when I went in. No wonder the cave was empty.

I left the cave and started walking toward the hills.

Unlike Japan proper, where the rainy season begins in June, it comes a month earlier in Okinawa.

Naturally, being a child at the time, I knew nothing about seasons, but I was conscious of how bad the weather continued to be. May being the rainy season, and my clothes wringing-wet from my experience in the cave, the night wind made me very cold. My teeth chattered, and I was hungry. I found a vegetable patch and felt under the potato plants to see if I could dig up any sweet potatoes and sure enough I found some small left-over ones. Hurriedly shaking off the earth I crammed them into my mouth. I also found some carrots and ate them, too.

Feeling myself again, I set off once more along the broad stony road. Since it was not yet dawn, it was thronged with refugees. Suddenly, the sound of machine-gun fire coincided with a rain of bullets. A stone right by my feet was smashed to fragments that flew into my legs. I started to run frantically, but the bullets never stopped whistling past my ears.

Just then, I caught sight of a house on the left side of the road surrounded by a stone wall. I tumbled down beside the wall for protection and crawled along it to the house. The house was empty, but for some reason, of the crowds of people running screaming down the road, not one thought of hiding in the house. Many of them fell, hit by bullets.

I hid in the house until the group of refugees had

gone by, thinking of how my father often cautioned me, "Tomiko, never just copy what other people do; always think things out for yourself." I remembered what I used to do when playing hide-and-seek: my secret was to avoid hiding near the others, for that was where the person who was "it" was bound to look. After that, I always made it a point to keep to myself as I fled.

The bullets finally stopped and everything became unbelievably quiet. I stayed in the house all day, and slept, and did not leave there until it was dark.

After walking a long time, I found myself on a wide road where I could see the sea on my left. I had no idea where I was. The road was muddy, and the canvas sports shoes I was wearing kept sticking in the mud. It was hard going as I picked my way, trying to avoid the worst places, and then right in front of me I saw a soldier lying in the road. Poor man, I thought, as I started to walk past him, he must have been killed by one of those bullets. By that time, I had seen so many dead bodies here and there that I had become quite used to the sight and was not frightened. But the soldier I thought was dead suddenly reached out his hand and grabbed hold of my ankle. As I let out a scream, he looked up at me with a grim expression and said, "Little girl, how's the war going?"

I thought for a moment, and then replied, "I think Japan's winning."

Whereupon, the terrible expression on his face gave way to a gentle smile.

"So we're winning. Thank you. Banzai!" he said in a

rather hoarse voice, letting go of my ankle. Then his face fell forward into the mud and he did not look up again, nor did he move any more.

I did not really know whether we were winning or losing the war. I was simply doing as my father had taught me. "Tomiko," he had said, "it doesn't matter what you hear or who tells you, you mustn't ever say that Japan is losing, even if you're wrong." But even if my father had not told me to do so, I don't think I could have had the heart to let down a dying soldier with bad news. Although I was in a desperate situation myself, I still wanted to comfort him.

I am still haunted, after these many years, by the memory of that soldier, grasping my ankle with his muddy hand and being so braced by the thought of the Japanese Army's superiority and his belief in Japan's victory that he could summon up his last reserves of strength to cry out "Banzai!" with his dying breath.

As I wandered about searching for my sisters, I saw many a soldier still gripping his gun or his sword or his bayonet as he lay dead.

I had no idea at the time what day of the month it was, but judging by the records, I think it must have been somewhere between the end of May and the beginning of June 1945. We left our home in Shuri as refugees on the twelfth or thirteenth of May, and must have reached Makabe about the fourteenth or fifteenth. We stayed there for several days, so it was probably about the nineteenth or twentieth when we arrived at Komesu beach where our brother died. And it may have been anywhere from the twenty-first to the twenty-fourth that I was separated from my sisters. That would make it somewhere between the twenty-seventh and the thirty-first that I found myself on the road under machine-gun attack and took refuge in the empty house with the stone wall. American Army assault records show that from May 31 to June 4 an attack was made from Tomigusuku Village and Kochinda Town in the west to the Minato River in the east.

I think now that I was separated from my sisters somewhere around Mabuni, east of Komesu beach, and the broad road where I encountered the machine-gun attack was the road to Tamagusuku Village, where I headed in the direction of Kochinda in my eagerness to press on. I was unwittingly going towards the action instead of away from it. This coincides with the American army records. I was, in fact, going northwards in a counterclockwise circle. Not a perfect circle, of course, since being only a little child not quite seven, who had no map or knowledge of geography, I simply zig-zagged around. That is why sometimes I would see the sea on my right and sometimes on my left. It seems certain that I was wandering around in the very center of the battle, which explains why I saw so many dead. Some days later, I came to a road I recognized. The four of us children had traveled together on this same road much earlier in our flight.

MY ANIMAL FRIENDS

The Ants

I had made up my mind to avoid people as much as possible and choose roads without many refugees. I thus became quite used to traveling alone and was not even afraid at night. It was far more frightening in the daytime when we were perfect targets for the enemy behind us to bombard, shoot and strafe. So I always found a cave to hide in in the daytime and only came out at night to look for food and to continue walking.

One night it was cloudy and very dark. I had become accustomed to seeing in the dark and had no trouble at all walking at night. On moonlit nights I could see almost as well as in the daytime, and starry nights were pretty good, too. But that night there was not a single star to see by. Feeling with my hands, I searched around in a grassy area for a vegetable patch, but couldn't find one anywhere. I had apparently stumbled into an area with nothing but pampas grass.

Presently, my foot was aware of a slight depression. When you can't see with your eyes, your hands and feet have to take over and you develop a sort of animal sense. As I sat down and carefully felt ahead of me with my toes, my foot dropped right down and I slid into a hollow that came up as high as my chest. Before I knew it, I was asleep.

Next morning I found that the pampas grass growing all around made a sort of roof over my hole. When I climbed out of the hole and looked around, I was completely surrounded by pampas grass as tall as I was. I found a little mound and stood on it, and jumped up in the air a few times to see if I could see anything that resembled a vegetable field, but there was nothing but pampas grass as far as the eye could see.

My stomach was rumbling because I had had nothing to eat since the morning before. I felt weak with hunger, so I went back into the hollow and curled up, holding my tummy. That was when I saw something that looked like a thin black string, moving. I looked closer and saw it was a line of ants, and each one was carrying something white in its mouth. Why, there must be something to eat nearby! I thought. How funny, on a pampas moor.

I followed the ants for about five or six yards and all became clear. There lay a soldier, and near him was his haversack, black with ants. The soldier must have been dead for some time, as he had begun to decompose. His belly was swollen up like a balloon, and there was a terrible smell. Steeling myself, I opened the lid of the haversack, and what did I find inside but my favorite sugar drops! When I took them out there were just enough to cover my palm. I put my hands together, as if to pray, and said softly, "Mr. Soldier, may I have these sweets? You're dead, so you won't be able to eat them." I gazed at the sugar drops for awhile, then I put two or three down for the ants. After that I said *"Itadakimasu,"* which means "I gratefully partake," a sort of grace we always say in Japan before eating. Then I put one of the sugar drops in my mouth and bit it. It was lovely and crunchy, and filled my mouth with sweetness.

That handful of candy pepped me up enormously. "Thank you, Mr. Soldier, thank you, ants" I said to myself. Henceforth, I always felt that dead soldiers were my friends, providing me with things to eat, and was no longer afraid of them, but I really was afraid of live soldiers. Those soldiers at Komesu beach had hardly allowed us any time at all to mourn our dear brother. I became skillful in deciding whether a soldier was alive or dead. Whenever I found one lying on the ground, I made quite sure first, from a distance, before running over to him. If a soldier did not react at all to the sound of a bomb or a shell, then he was dead and it was safe to approach him. If he moved a hand or leg or any part of his body at the sound of a bomb bursting, he was still alive. Once, though, I made a dreadful mistake.

I was quite sure the soldier was dead and after folding my hands politely in prayer, I had stretched out my hand to partake of what was in his haversack, when I felt a large hand on my shoulder. Letting out a little scream I said, "Oh, I am sorry" and fell over backwards. I was so frightened I couldn't move for some time, and just lay there trembling. But in spite of it all, I was so hungry that I went back and put my hand in his haversack. There were sugar-drops, hard biscuits, and a can of salmon.

I managed to make a small hole in the lid of the can by pressing it hard against a pointed stone. But the stone became blunt in the process, so I found another stone and made the hole a little bigger. When the hole was big enough, I managed to get the contents out by using two twigs like chopsticks. As far as I remember I had never been shown how to open a can, but somehow, extreme hunger taught me what to do.

The reason the pampas moor I had strayed into was completely devoid of people was that you could see right into it from the air; it was no good as a hiding place. There was nobody there but me, the dead soldier, and some small animals that had taken refuge from the noise of the bombing and shelling. A goat, startled by a bomb, tore right past me through the pampas grass, and I could see American planes over the valley dropping bombs, soon followed by terrific explosions that rocked the ground.

The Rat's Gift

It was now broad daylight and I thought I might become a target, so I looked around frantically for a hole to hide in. But no matter how I searched among the pampas grass, there was not a hole to be found anywhere. Then I remembered that my father had once said, "If you are fated to die, it doesn't matter where you go, you're bound to die. And if you're meant to live, you'll survive all sorts of dangers." So I gave up my frantic search. I decided that if I was going to die anyway, I might as well enjoy myself as much as possible, and that it would be better to die in the fresh air than in one of those smelly caves. And besides, what was the use of finding a cave that was so full of people already that they drove you away? After all, I had got into the habit of avoiding people and keeping to myself.

And yet, I didn't like the idea of dying there in the pampas moor like that soldier and becoming a weather-beaten skeleton. Wondering where it would be best to die, I made up my mind to find a hole of my own after all. A small one would do.

After searching for a long time, I finally found a small opening in the ground. But even as I prepared to die, food became the next priority. I had eaten all the food that belonged to the soldier and no matter how I searched I could not find so much as the tail end of a sweet potato. I wondered if I would die in this hole, and the thought that nobody would ever find me suddenly filled me with sadness. I thought of my strict father and my sweet mother, and my sisters Yoshiko and Hatsuko who went so far as to slap my cheek in their anxiety that I should eat my rice, and Nini, who always used to play with me. One by one their faces passed before me in my mind. How nice and warm my father's broad back had felt when he carried me piggyback! And my mother's lovely lullabies! The thought of my parents gave me a moment or two of calm.

It was just then that I saw a rat carrying a small sweet potato in its front paws. When it saw me, it was so startled it dropped the sweet potato and scuttled away. I was startled too, but I was so hungry I picked up the sweet potato, saying, "Oh, you nice mousie!" and after scraping off the rat's tooth-marks on a nearby stone I sank my teeth ravenously into it.

"Thank you, Mr. Rat," I said, when I had gobbled it up. Not only was I grateful to him for the sweet potato, but for his letting me know that there was a vegetable plot nearby.

Once again I was filled with the courage to go on living. I must find that vegetable plot, I said to myself, then I can eat some more sweet potatoes!

Nini the Rabbit

I set off the next day, but no matter where I went, the pampas moor just stretched on endlessly, with nothing even remotely resembling a field of vegetables. It began to rain, and I knew I would soon become drenched if I didn't find another cave.

Then, ahead of me, I saw a clump of pampas that was taller than the rest, and down by its roots was a hole. Thank goodness, I thought, and slid into it, landing on my backside with a thud. As I did so, I felt something warm under me. Oh dear, I said to myself, I've sat down on a dying soldier! I lifted my bottom ever so gingerly and peeked.

It was a white rabbit!

A broad expanse of pampas grass, with no sight of a hole to hide in.

Maybe it was someone's lost pet rabbit? It was look-ing up at me with its crimson eyes, twitching its whiskers, wriggling its nose, and trembling. It seemed terrified by the continual noise of exploding bombs and shells, for it made no attempt to run away when I appeared.

"Sorry to come in suddenly like that. I must have hurt you," I said, stroking its back. The rabbit laid back its long ears and blinked. Every time a bomb burst it flinched, and gave a shudder.

"It's all right. Those bombs are bursting over in the valley. That one was a long way off."

I held the rabbit in my arms and spoke to it every time there was an explosion. Talking to it made me feel better too. The rabbit felt so nice and soft and warm in my arms. After a while, the rabbit stopped trembling.

"There now, that's better isn't it? You must have

been awfully scared. Let's go to sleep together now, like this, okay?"

Of course the rabbit didn't answer, but it was wonderful to have someone to talk to once more. I soon began to feel drowsy and before I knew it I was fast asleep.

I dreamed about Nini, my brother who died at Komesu. He was holding my hand and wanting me to go somewhere to play. On the way we came to a rushing stream and I was afraid to cross it, and cried. But Nini held my hand tightly and said, "It's all right, Tomiko. I'm here with you. Just be brave and we'll cross together," and he put his arm around me and got me safely to the other side. Then we came to a large meadow covered with yellow mustard flowers, and I was so happy I shrieked with joy as we played about. Then it began to get dark, and Nini said, "Mommy will be worried, so we'd better be going home."

"I don't want to go yet," I demurred, "I'm thirsty. I want a drink of water."

"Oh, shucks. Well, all right. Try this. You eat it this way," said Nini, and picked a stalk of bamboo or pampas—I don't know what it was exactly—some kind of edible plant that grew nearby, and showed me how to munch it.

"The juice is sweet. Try it."

I ate the piece he handed me, but it didn't have any taste at all. Then the scene changed and we were on the road home and came to that rushing stream once more.

"Give me your hand, Tomiko. Now, hold on tightly to mine."

I clutched Nini's hand for all I was worth, when suddenly the current became stronger and my feet felt as if they would be carried away. I screamed, "Nini, I'm scared!"

My own scream woke me up. I was clutching the rabbit's forelegs with all my strength, and its head was wet with my tears.

It occurred to me then that Mother had felt sorry for me in my lonesome state and had sent Nini to me in the guise of the rabbit. Yes! That was it.

I had no idea how long I had been in that hole. I peeked outside and found the rain had cleared completely, and the moon was shining.

I decided to call the rabbit Nini. Neither of us had anything to eat, so I thought I would pick some grass for him, and there in among the pampas near our hole I suddenly noticed a weed that looked exactly like the kind that my brother had shown me how to eat in my dream. I crawled out and picked some and put it in my mouth, and lo and behold, I found my mouth filled with a sweet juice!

It was fantastic. Just as my brother Nini had said in my dream, the leaves of the weed were delicious. I picked some of the tenderest-looking leaves for Nini the rabbit, who munched them with gusto.

"Let's stick it out together, Nini, to the end," I said. "We can live on this. And we don't need swords or guns to protect ourselves with. After all, theirs didn't protect those soldiers from being killed." I had seen more dead soldiers than I could count.

Nini gazed up at my mouth as I ate. He was probably trying to tell me that he wanted something more to eat. But to me it seemed as if he were my dead brother saying, "That's right, Tomiko, you eat that grass and stay alive."

Nini Saves My Life

I made up my mind I would find some carrots for Nini. I wanted to take Nini with me, but being white, I was afraid he would be too conspicuous in the moonlight. And besides, it would have been too cruel if he were killed a second time, having already died once at Komesu.

"Wait for me here, Nini," I said. "I'm going to find you some nice carrots. Be good, now, and don't go out."

I put Nini the rabbit as far back as possible in the hole and stuffed the entrance with pampas grass, and then I tied some stalks of pampas together as a landmark, so I could find the place when I came back.

I had not gone very far when I saw in the distance what looked like a field. As I made my way through the pampas, I kept repeating over and over to myself the words "Carrots, carrots," as if they were a magic formula. The pampas grass suddenly gave way, and there was the field.

But what should I see right in the middle of the field but a human-like figure. It was white, and swaying around. A ghost, I thought, and dropped to the ground.

But then, looking carefully, I saw that what I thought was a ghost was the top half of man clad in the sort of white cotton undershirt soldiers wear. He was bending forward, writhing in agony. When I looked closer to see why he was doing so, I saw that he was cutting his own belly with a short sword, but he had not yet died and was in great pain. I could hear him groaning. And then I noticed another soldier holding a long Japanese sword. He went behind the writhing, swaying soldier and put his hands together and prayed, then he moved to one side and I saw the blade of his sword flash in the light of the moon.

Suddenly, I was terrified, and turned and ran as fast as my legs would carry me. I didn't want to risk being discovered.

I had no idea what was going on. It was not until years later that I understood that one of the soldiers had been committing hara-kiri and the other assisting him by cutting off his head to put him out of his misery. At the time, I was startled, and very frightened.

I found another field, where I dug up some carrots and hurried back with them to the hole where Nini was. But the hole was empty. Where could he be? And here I had brought him his favorite carrots. I was suddenly very upset. Could he by chance have followed me? I retraced my path back through the pampas, softly calling, "Nini! Nini!"

But although I went all the way back to the field where I had dug up the carrots, I could find no sign of Nini. Just then, there was a terrific explosion behind me.

I turned around and saw that the entire area around the hole where Nini and I had found solace had turned bright red. The pampas grass was a sea of flames. An incendiary bomb had landed right by our hole. The object of an incendiary bomb is to destroy buildings and vegetation, so it is made to burn everything within a fixed radius with a very intense heat.

If Nini had been there in the hole when I got back, and if I hadn't gone out to look for him, I would have perished in that inferno. Animals are said to have a sixth sense that warns them of danger. I believed Nini's premonition of the incendiary bomb had saved my life. I was profoundly grateful to Nini. But at the same time, I felt terribly sad to have lost my dear little companion. "I hope you're alive somewhere and that you're all right, Nini," I said, leaving one of the carrots for him in the hope that he would find it if he was still alive. And I said a little prayer.

FROM CAVE TO CAVE

"If You Want to Escape, Now's the Time!"

The tiny little home in the pampas moor, where I had spent one night with Nini, had been burned to a cinder. Dreaming of my brother made me long to find my sisters and be with them again.

As the morning sky began to grow light, I left the still smoldering and sputtering pampas behind and set off once more. Thinking my sisters would probably have taken refuge in a cave, I started down into the valley towards a cliff that looked as if it might have some caves in it. As I made my way down around the rocky outcrops, I could clearly make out several caves in the valley, half-way down the cliff face.

"I have a feeling I'm going to find them there," I said to myself as I carefully stepped between the rocks, wending my way along the cliff towards the caves.

Looking down at one of the caves from above, I could see some soldiers lying near the entrance. But it was too steep to reach that cave from where I was. Wondering how I could get there, I leaned as far out as I could, to see if there was a safe way down, and as I did so, I accidentally dislodged some rocks that went rumbling down on top of the soldiers.

"Oh my goodness!"

I held my breath. There was nowhere I could go or hide. There was nothing I could do but stand my ground, waiting for the rebuke. But although there were at least three or four soldiers there, not one stood up or spoke.

"They're dead. I'm saved!" I said out loud without thinking. It was a dreadful thing to say, but I couldn't help it, since I was afraid of soldiers. Dead soldiers, however, were a different matter.

When I had regained my composure, I picked my way

slowly down the cliff by a roundabout route to where the soldiers were. There were four of them and they were, in fact, dead. But their faces looked so peaceful, just as if they were sleeping. There was one haversack lying nearby. Quite naturally, I felt inside it with my hand. There were only five or six tiny sugar-drops. I put two or three in my mouth and as I crunched them I took a look inside the cave, whose entrance was half blocked up.

Near the opening I could see a little girl about my own age sitting on a woman's lap. The little girl noticed me eating and stared at my mouth. As I crunched, she moved her own mouth in unison.

"Oh, you'd like some, too, wouldn't you?" I crawled into the cave and gave her the last one. Then I looked into the dark recesses of the cave and tried calling, "Nene, Nene!" But there was no reply.

They aren't here. I'll have to try another cave, I thought. Then it occurred to me that if I stayed here they might come. Moreover, I was tired. I would stay. I squatted down near the entrance with my arms clasped around my knees. Then someone spoke from the back of the cave.

"Little girl, if you want to escape, now's the time. We're going to seal the entrance and blow ourselves up with a bomb. Of course, you can die along with us if you like."

A shiver went right through me. I sprang out of the cave and slid down the cliff, trying to get as far away as I could. Presently, there was a loud explosion behind me, which echoed around the valley. I never knew whether the sound came from that cave or whether it was an American army shell. I was too frightened to find out.

During the war in caves throughout Okinawa many fleeing mothers with their children felt so exhausted and hopeless that they took their own lives. I can still picture the faint smile that lit up the face of that little girl when I shared my sugar-drop with her.

The Chase

I became so weary looking for my sisters that once while I was hiding behind a rock I fell asleep. Awaking with a start, I looked around and was struck by the peculiar fact that there was not a single ant anywhere to be seen. I was filled with sudden terror. Nini the rabbit's disappearance had taught me that when I saw no animals it meant a bomb was about to drop. I learned never to set out before making sure that there were creatures about such as ants, butterflies, lizards or mice. If I could see no living things around me, I knew I must get away from there in a hurry, while if there were living creatures around, I felt I could breathe freely and look inside caves, calling, "Nene, Nene!"

I went from cave to cave, day after day. But no matter how many caves I visited, here, there and everywhere, I obtained no news of my sisters. It soon became an obsession, and being determined to find Yoshiko and Hatsuko, I would set out from a cave while it was still light to continue the search. Eventually, people hiding in caves got so they resented my daylight forays because it made me an enemy target. I became known as a bad urchin they didn't want around. Sometimes, when I approached a cave I was told, "Don't come here! Go away!" and I was not even allowed to look inside. Since I often found myself back at a cave I had been to before, I naturally became quite well known. But wanting very badly to find my beloved sisters, I didn't care.

I had some terrifying experiences during this time. When I arrived at maybe my fifth cave, I peered inside and was just about to call out the names of my sisters, when suddenly, a soldier came at me brandishing a Japanese sword. He shouted at me, with a savage look on his face, "It's too dangerous to let you live. I'm going to kill you!"

I was flabbergasted. My father, and the soldiers at the Signal Corps unit had always told me that soldiers were there to protect us, and here was one raising his sword to kill me!

I ran for dear life. I could run quite fast for my age, and the soldier had trouble keeping up with me, but he was too hard on my heels for me to shake him off. I kept looking around me for somewhere to hide, but there was nowhere.

I was finally driven to the edge of a steep cliff. Beyond me was a deep valley, and below me a precipice that appeared dizzyingly sheer to my childish eyes. If I jumped, I was bound to die. Behind me was a soldier with a sword in his hand getting closer every moment. It meant certain death either way. The situation was hopeless.

Still, I looked for a way out. Then I suddenly spied a small rock jutting out right below me and thinking it would at least take me a step further away, I jumped out onto it.

Turning around, I saw the soldier's flushed face just above mine. Not only could I hear his heavy breathing, but I could feel it on my face. With a grunt, he brought down his heavy Japanese sword, it's blade flashing. "It's going to cut me!" I thought, and resigned myself to the fact that I only had a moment left to live. I was not the least bit afraid. Strangely, the thing that came to my mind was the hara-kiri scene I had witnessed in the field by the pampas moor, and I thought how much this sword flashing just now above my head resembled the sword brandished by the soldier who was completing the act for the one who had disemboweled himself. All this only took one moment, of course, but for me, time seemed to have stopped.

Just as the sword was about to cut me down, the rock underneath me broke off. The rock and I tumbled straight down towards the bottom of the cliff, and I lost consciousness.

Saved by a Fluke

I don't know how long it was before I suddenly came to. I felt as if I was floating, and dangling in the air. "Where am I?" I wondered, and when I reached out for something I could hold onto, there was nothing there. I kicked my legs, but they didn't make contact with anything. The worst thing was that something hard, like a stick seemed to be poking into my stomach. "What is it?" I wondered, and when I felt with my hand I discovered it was the tip of a tree. I was hanging face up, caught on a tree by the front of my work pants. The tree was growing out of the cliff partway down.

The last moments before I lost consciousness gradually came back to me. I had been saved by the only tree growing in the area. There was nothing left of the tree except its trunk and main branches. It had no small branches or leaves. It appeared to be a dead tree.

"I've been saved. God has saved me. It must be Daddy and Mommy and Nini's doing. I've got to go on living now!" I took hold of the tree trunk and pulled myself up onto it as if it were a horizontal gymnastics bar. But all I could see below me was the valley, and above me was the steep cliff—and not a single other tree anywhere near.

"Here I am, saved, but how am I going to get down?"

Once again I was filled with despair and felt it would have been just as well had I been cut down with that Japanese sword.

"Well, I've got to do something." I twisted my body around and stretched my arm along the trunk of the tree to see if there was anything behind me that I could hold onto. As I did so, there was a loud creak, and the tree tumbled down to the bottom of the valley with me hanging onto it. The tree had so decayed that it was not even able to support the weight of a child.

The sky and the cliff and the bottom of the valley

swam round and round before my eyes as I fell, somersaulting over and over. Finally my body came to rest with a bump. I could see the sky. I could see the cliff. And quite a long way up it, I could see a small landslide, marking the path of my fall. And all down the slope at the bottom of the cliff were marks where something had dropped and then bounced along. The bounce marks stretched right along to where I was lying.

"My goodness! Did I fall all that way?" I lay there for some time looking up at the line of crumbled earth.

Before long, I felt pain in my knees. When I looked, I saw that my work pants were torn to shreds and my knees, which were poking through, were bleeding. Wiping the blood away with my fingers, I found that the wounds were full of gravel. My whole body ached, and I discovered that only the top button was left on my jacket. All the other buttons were gone. I had also lost the padded air-raid bonnet I had been wearing all the time. And my sneakers must have come off, too, for I was barefoot.

"I look like an old rag," I said to myself.

I lay down on some cold, damp fallen leaves and went to sleep.

A River of Death

I was wakened by the sound of running water. It was quite dark, but I knew the moon would soon be out, because I could see a faint glow at the edge of the cliff.

"There's a river nearby. That's wonderful, 'cause I'm

thirsty." Rather unsteadily, I shuffled in the direction of the sound. Miraculously, no bones seemed to be broken. The sound of the running water came closer and closer.

"There! I was right. It's a river."

A little beyond me flowed a mountain stream, but I did not approach it straight away. Experience had taught me to be cautious. Should a soldier recognize me and chase me again, this time it would surely be the end. I decided to hide behind a boulder on the riverbed, a little way off, and study the situation.

I could not see any soldiers, but many ordinary people, lying on their stomachs on the bank drinking the water. All those people would stir up the water and make it muddy, so I decided to wait until they were gone and the river cleared.

When was it last that I had had a drink of nice, clean water? I waited my turn. Beside the sugar-drops, the can of salmon and the hard biscuits that were in the dead soldiers' haversacks, all I had had to eat since being separated from my sisters were raw sweet potatoes and carrots, and when I was thirsty I had sucked the juice of the grass that Nini had shown me in my dream and sipped off the clear part of rain water caught in rock crevices.

Although I waited and waited, none of the drinkers lifted their faces from the river.

They must be frightfully thirsty, I thought.

I could not wait any longer, and decided to go over to the river. Just then, one of the people lying on their stomachs raised their head and looked in my direction.

It was an old crone with wildly disheveled hair. When I saw her face I involuntarily let out a scream and sprang back a step or two. Blood was running down from one eye and her body was crimson from cheek to chest. She neither stretched out her hand to me nor called out, but sank back into the water with a splash and did not move again. I knew, then, that all those people with their faces in the river were dead.

I made my way slowly and cautiously to the river bank. The moon had just come out and I could see my way clearly. But I could no longer dart about as I used to. I was now barefoot, having lost my sneakers when I fell, and had to pick my way with care to avoid injury.

Among the people lying on the banks of the river were soldiers which I had not noticed before, old men, and mothers with dead children clinging to their backs. Corpses were floating out in the river, too, being slowly carried downstream, some caught up on rocks here and there in the current. I think now there must have been about a hundred altogether.

I saw a young woman with her hair in braids like my sister Yoshiko used to wear. What if it were she? I ran over and peered into her face, but it was someone quite different.

I could not possibly have drunk the water there. I began walking in the upstream direction, past masses of corpses. What I saw is impossible to find words to describe. It was like an artist's depiction of hell. There were people as far as the eye could see, and yet not the sound of a single human voice, for they were all dead. It was a most oppressive silence. The only sounds were the flowing stream and the footsteps of the one living soul—me. How weird the pitter-patter of my own footsteps sounded, as if there might be someone else alive after all.

Eventually there were no more corpses and the river became clear. Now for that drink, I thought, but when I bent down and put my hand in the water I recoiled in horror. It was wriggling with maggots. They were not only on the surface, but lower down, and on the bottom, too. "How horrid," I thought, quickly withdrawing my hand. I stared at the maggots for a while. They were everywhere. But my throat was parched and if I did not get a drink here I did not know when I might have another chance. I boldly put both hands in, and pushing the maggots aside, I scooped up some water and drank it.

"My! That's good!" I said out loud without thinking. Wanting some more, I got down on all fours and pushing the maggots aside with my hands I put my mouth in the river and drank and drank. When I had finished, I wiped something away that was tickling my mouth and chin, and four or five maggots fell into the water. They had crawled up my arms as I was drinking. But I didn't care. It was the first time in ages that I had been able to drink my fill of water.

A FATEFUL MEETING

The Cave

After crawling away from the river of death I began walking again, but without a purpose. Not having found my sisters after all my searching, I lost hope. Wherever I went, there were corpses strewn all over, and I felt certain that my sisters, too, were dead. I decided to concentrate on staying alive so that I could bury Nini's remains in the family grave as Yoshiko had wanted. These thoughts filled me with sadness, for I now came to the conclusion that I was the only one left.

I began to avoid the vicinity of caves as much as possible and kept to pampas moors, overgrown fields, thickets and groves of trees. I could find more to eat there, and there was less chance of running across scary soldiers.

I had been walking for quite a time when I suddenly found myself in a familiar place. "I've been here before!" Yes! Here I was going along in a completely hit-or-miss way, and I had come back to the place where Yoshiko, Hatsuko and Chokuyu and I had all fled together. I was somewhere near Komesu Beach. Oddly, while the road then had been jammed with refugees, now there was not a person to be seen. There was hardly anyone on the beach, either, in spite of the fact that behind me could be heard the continuous sound of explosions and the rat-a-tat-tat of machine-gun fire. I had advanced towards the action at one point, then turned to escape the bursting bombs and shells by fleeing southwards again. And now with the enemy on my heels I had once more come to the southernmost tip of Okinawa's main island. Much later, I figured out that it must have been somewhere between the fifteenth and seventeenth of June. According to the United States Army's records of their advance, on June 11 they held a line from the town of Itoman on the southwest coast past central Mount Yaese to the village of Gushikami on the southeast coast. By the nineteenth they had

A broad, stony road, surrounded by fields, once used by countless fleeing refugees.

advanced almost as far south as Mabuni.

Judging by these dates, I must have entered the pampas moor about the third or fourth of June, and my narrow escape from death at the hands of the soldier brandishing the sword must have taken place sometime between the sixth and eighth. I am still not sure where that valley I fell into was but think it must have been in the middle reaches of the Mukue River, which rises in Kochinda and flows into the sea past the town of Itoman. I probably wandered eight or nine days after I got away from the river of death, which would make it somewhere between the fifteenth and the seventeenth that I reached the southern tip of Okinawa.

Thus, five weeks would have elapsed since I left my home in Shuri, which means that I had been wandering about alone in the midst of the battle for nearly a month.

To see the ocean again—the blue, blue sea—as I gazed at it from my hiding place, filled me with no emotions at all. I was just simply tired. And I was hungry. I had failed to find my sisters. I had now even lost my determination to bury Nini's remains in our family tomb.

"I don't think I want to go on living," I muttered to myself as I gazed at the sea stretching away before my eyes.

It was strange, but I saw no enemy ships on the sea, nor any airplanes in the sky. Perhaps it was just that for those few moments none happened to enter my field of vision. The sea looked so peaceful it was hard to believe that it was part of a battle hell.

The sea at the southern tip of Okinawa.

"As long as I'm going to die, I think I'll find a nice little cave and go to sleep in it. I haven't eaten for three days, so I'll probably die in my sleep."

I left the beach and walked about in an area where I thought there were likely to be caves, and looked for a suitably small one.

Presently, I came upon one whose entrance looked just big enough for me to squeeze through. As I placed my hand on the side of the cave, I noticed some *nigana* growing on a nearby rock.

"Why, that's the leaf Daddy once ate in his field!"

I stretched out my hand and picked some and crammed it into my mouth.

"Gosh, it"s bitter."

In spite of my hunger, the bitterness made it unpalatable.

"Tomiko, if you eat this it will make you healthy," I seemed to hear my father saying. But my mouth tasted so bitter I thirsted for water. So even though I was intending to die I went in search of some.

Not wanting to retrace my steps to the coast, I set off in the opposite direction. After I had gone a little way, I came across a small opening in the ground overgrown with bracken.

"A spring!" I cried aloud, anticipating a satisfying draught of sparkling water. On my trips with Father to help him in his field, we would often pass places on the path overgrown with large bracken plants where there were clear water springs. Whenever I passed one I always made a point to stop and drink the water as it spurted out.

I ran over eagerly and parted the bracken. But it was not a spring. It was merely a hole in the ground. However, a most delicious aroma emanated from its depths. What kind of a hole could this be? I put my face near the opening and peered in, but it was so dark I could see nothing at all. But I could still smell the mouth-watering aroma. It was just like Mother's scrumptious miso soup.

Yes, that's what it was! I was unable to contain myself any longer. I decided to investigate. I couldn't see what was down there, but if it was something to eat, it couldn't be dangerous. But how to climb in? The hole was only just big enough for me to squeeze through. Yes, that's it, I thought, I'll go in feet first. I remembered my father saying that one's head is the most valuable part of one's body, so one must always take care of it. "If you're not sure what's ahead of you," he used to say, "feel with your feet."

So I let my feet down first. But they just dangled in midair. Resting my hands on the rim of the hole to support myself, I let myself down a little further and moved my feet around in a circle until I felt the bottom. Now I was all right. I could let go with my hands. When I was down on the bottom, I found the cave was larger than I expected. I looked around but could not see what was there.

Finally, as my eyes became accustomed to the dark, I could make out the inside of the cave. I was in a level tunnel about four and a half feet in diameter, two or three yards in from the opening. It sloped down gradually ahead of me for about three yards, at the end of which was a flat area about nine feet wide, twelve feet deep, and four and a half feet high. The only light was the little that filtered down from the hole I had just entered.

Then I saw what I thought was a person sitting with his back against the rock wall. When I looked harder, I saw it was an old man, and he was watching me intently. Oh dear! I thought, am I going to be chased away again? What shall I do? Quickly, I gave the old man a friendly smile.

"Come over here, child," said the old man, in a kind voice.

It was all right! I heaved a sigh of relief.

"Who were you talking to?" The voice came from someone on his left. When I looked in that direction I saw that there was a little old woman as thin as a scarecrow sitting quietly near the old man a bit farther inside the cave.

I accepted the old man's invitation and went over to them.

"Well, won't you sit down?" said the old man.

"Yes, thank you" I said, and squatted down on my heels in front of the old man, clasping my knees. I sat this way in case he should tell me to leave, so that I could get up quickly. It was a habit of sitting I had acquired just to be on the safe side.

That is when I noticed for the first time that the old man's body was not quite normal. Both his arms had been amputated at the elbows and both his legs at the knees. Why, he looks just like a *daruma*, I thought to myself. (*Daruma* dolls have no arms or legs and are representations of the Indian Buddhist monk Dharma, who meditated in a cave so long that his limbs atrophied.)

Where the old man's limbs had been amputated, the stumps were bound with white cloth onto which blood had oozed through here and there. I was horrified to see maggots wriggling about on the cloth. He looked a pitiful figure. As for the old woman, she appeared to be blind. For although she was looking toward me, she never moved her head or her eyes.

The old man asked me my name.

"I'm Tomiko Matsukawa," I replied. "And I'm six years old."

Thinking about it now, if it was somewhere around the sixteenth of June, I would have just turned seven, since my birthday was June fourteenth. But I had lost all sense of time.

"And how do you come to be here?" he asked.

"I came from Shuri." I explained, "with my sisters Yoshiko and Hatsuko and my brother Chokuyu. But my brother was killed by a bullet at Komesu. Yoshiko and Hatsuko and I buried him with sand. Then the three of us escaped to the hills. But I've lost Yoshiko and Hatsuko. After that I have been sleeping in the fields and looking for my sisters but I couldn't find them anywhere. I was walking along and found this hole."

"What became of your father and your mother?"

"Father went to Makabe on Signal Corps business, but he didn't come back. He told us that if he didn't come home we were to talk it over and decide what was best to do. So Yoshiko decided we should go towards the south. My mother died a long time ago."

That brief outline was about the best that I could manage as a seven year old. While I was speaking, the old man nodded, saying "Yes, yes, I see," while the old woman said, "Poor thing," and wiped her eyes with her kimono sleeve, when I spoke of the death of Nini and my mother.

"Well, well. So that's what happened. You're a good girl. And now you don't need to go anywhere else. You can stay here with us."

When I heard his words I flopped down onto my bottom with relief. Up to that moment, I had been shooed away from more caves than I could count, just as if I had been a dog or a cat. I was so terribly happy that even though I knew it was bad manners, I thrust out my legs in front of me as I used to do at home.

"You must be pretty hungry." said the old man. "There's some food on the shelf. You can help yourself. But don't eat too much at once. The war may go on a long time. And don't talk too loud, because a spy might find out about us and throw a bomb in here."

Peace Among the Three of Us

The cave was mostly in its natural state, except for one wall, which seemed to have been scraped flat by hand. From that wall was suspended a shelf consisting of a raft of short logs, the size of kindling, tied together. On the shelf were such staples as a bunch of dried kelp, a jar of brown sugar, and a jar of dried soy beans, and from one corner of the shelf hung a cluster of three or four dried bonito fillets. Below, half buried in the ground, was an earthenware crock containing miso relish, and beside the old man was a pot of salt. Under a spot where a spring seeped through a crack in the wall stood a brown earthenware jar brimming with lovely clear water, and a ladle lay across the rim of the jar.

After having roughed it in the open for a month, this cave seemed like a dream palace. I had no reservations at all about wanting to stay there forever, and strived to be an obedient child.

The first thing I did each day was to take a pinch of salt from the pot the old man kept beside him and let it into his wounds through the bandages. I also picked off the maggots. And sometimes, when I saw him screw up his face as if he had an itch somewhere, I would scratch the place for him, and he would lean back against the wall of the cave and begin snoring gently with relief. Sometimes I would rub the skin near his red, swollen sores with the ball of my finger. Where white pus had collected, I would squeeze with all my might and get it out, and put salt there. An expression of pain would cross his face, but he never complained, and simply gazed into the distance, bearing it with fortitude.

"Tomiko," he would say, looking at me with such loving kindness, "I'm going to get better because of you. You've saved my life. I used to get Granny to scratch me where I itched, but because she's blind, I couldn't ask her very often. So I'd scratch the place against the wall, but it hurt when I touched the sores. And when those doggone maggots used to bite my sores, I just couldn't stand the pain. I'd try to get them off by rubbing them against the wall, but once those little devils get their teeth into you they won't let go. But now Tomiko, with her dear little fingers, gets rid of them for me, and it feels very good. I'm grateful."

Sometimes a slight tear would stain his face when he spoke like that.

At mealtimes I would get the food down from the shelf and divide it according to Granny's instructions. I used to feed Grandpa, because he could not feed himself. I would shred the kelp and the bonito into small pieces for him, and put them in his mouth. After he had eaten kelp or miso he would drink lots of water. Bringing him the water from the water jar was another of my duties.

Grandpa was very fond of miso relish, and used to ask for that first. I would give him a mouthful and he would half close his eyes as he munched it, just the way Nini the rabbit did. It was awfully sweet the way Grandpa opened wide his mouth when I fed him, just like a baby. His whiskers used to tickle my fingers and make me giggle, which in turn made Grandpa laugh, too.

In spite of having lost both hands and feet, the old man seemed strong and healthy. His pallor was due either to having been so long in the cave and out of the sunlight, or due to having lost a lot of blood through his wounds. Still, he had a handsome mustache, a full chest and broad, sturdy shoulders. Above all, his posture was magnificent, and he always sat up straight.

The miso relish had large pieces of pork in it as well as ginger and brown sugar and was absolutely delicious. Every house has its own recipe for making miso relish and there is always a subtle difference between them. This old couple's miso relish was very like the miso relish my mother used to make, and my! It was good. The old lady must have made it before losing her eyesight.

She was a lady of great beauty and refinement. Except for her eyesight she was uninjured, and was able to look after herself. But she was just skin and bones and seemed rather weak. She asked for some bonito, and when I handed her a largish piece, she dropped it. And when she drank water, she tended to spill it on her lap unless I held the cup. Her teeth were not very good, either, so it took her a long time to eat. We were not able to cook in the cave, so all we had was preserved food, mostly dried, and therefore hard. So I would chew things like bonito flakes for her first, to soften them.

"Oh, how lovely and soft these bonito flakes are! Thank you." she would say, with a little bow, turning her sightless eyes towards me.

The old lady, not being strong, spent most of the time lying down. She was always saying how cold she was, and she would pull up an old ragged cloth she kept by her side. I found a worn kimono belonging to the old man and put it over her.

"What a kind child you are, Tomiko. How I wish I could see your face," she said, stretching out her skinny hand and finding my cheek, and stroking it. "Ah, you look just the way I imagined," she went on. "You have such a sweet face. If only I could see." A tear fell from the corner of her half-closed eyes.

She had a wonderful memory, and even if she could not see, she remembered where everything was. She would say things like, "Tomiko, bring me the jar of brown sugar. It's the second from the right on the shelf." She never once made a mistake. It was she, no doubt, who had someone partially bury the miso crock in the ground, for burying the crock preserves the miso from going bad.

It was the first time in a long while that I had not had to keep on walking, had not been driven away from caves, and had not had to search for something to eat in dead soldiers' haversacks. It was truly a time of rest and peace of mind for me.

Although the Pacific War continued outside the cave, and the fighting was very fierce as the war approached its tragic end, our cave was a haven of peace in the battle area. How blessed we were! But how long could it last? When I finished my ministrations to the old couple, I used to savor moments of deep happiness.

On the other hand, the unforgettable scenes of horror that I had witnessed since being parted from my sisters kept coming back to haunt me. One of these experiences had occurred on a night when I was searching for my sisters. All was quiet except for the sound of the wind. I had discovered a cave, and crouching down I tiptoed towards the entrance. Inside, I heard a baby crying, the sound becoming gradually louder. I quickly hid, and watched the entrance to the cave. Soon, a young mother with a screaming infant on her back appeared, being pushed out of the cave by four or five soldiers. The young mother pointed towards the inside of the cave, bowing over and over again to the soldiers. She seemed to be begging them to let her return to the cave, but they were adamant, and drove her out. She stood near the entrance for some time, then gave up hope and walked away, hanging her head.

"Oh, how dangerous, to walk along like that!" I said to myself, and just then, a machine gun went rat-a-tat-tat and she spun round like a top and dropped to the ground. She did not move any more, but the baby on her back continued to cry. Then I saw a black shadow come out of the cave, crawl along the ground to where she lay, pull off the baby from her back and hurry behind a rock. The baby's cries gradually became more distant and then suddenly stopped altogether. The cave was silent again, the only sound being the rustling of the trees in the wind.

I was not brave enough to take another look inside that cave. I slowly backed away and left the place, setting off to find some other cave.

Two or three nights after that, I was cautiously approaching a cave when I saw about fifteen soldiers lying in a row on the rocky area in front of the entrance while a soldier wearing a sword, who I thought must be an officer, was pacing about near them. I wondered what was going on, and hid behind a large tree and watched. The soldiers lying on the ground appeared to be rather badly wounded and did not move much. Mixed with a low moaning like the doleful howls of a dog, I could hear various shouts. There were cries of "Help! Help!" and a hoarse "Kill 'em quickly!" followed by the plea, "Put me out of my misery as soon as you can!" that seemed to be wrung from the depths of torment. Gasping for breath, someone called out, "Mother!" and someone else, "Good-bye" followed by a woman's name. The cries were so pathetic I could hardly bear to listen.

"I'm sorry. There aren't enough bullets. I'll have to do it this way." The officer with the long sword at his waist took a short sword from one of the soldiers and started stabbing the wounded soldiers, plunging his blade into the left side of their throats. Each let out a strangled cry, and fell back limp and still.

"I'm sorry. I'm sorry. Forgive me!" said the officer, as he continued stabbing one soldier after the other in the throat.

Then one or two called out, "Stop! Stop! Leave us alone!" and began to cry, and some even tried to crawl away and escape, whereupon the officer's movements became faster and faster as he leapt from one to the other, raising his sword like a hatchet, just like a wild animal attacking its prey.

I was well aware of the reason for this cruelty. It was because the moaning of the wounded soldiers would be heard by the enemy and provoke a fierce shower of machine-gun fire. I knew, because when I had gone from cave to cave calling out for my sisters in a loud voice, one soldier guarding a cave said, "Shut up, urchin, the enemy'll hear you. And it won't be just you who gets killed, but all of us in the cave. Go away! Shoo!" Then I had finally been chased by the soldier with the sword and very nearly killed.

Yet it seemed unthinkable to me that one of our own soldiers could kill a defenseless mother, a small child like me, or a baby, just to save his own skin.

War makes people crazy. That mother might have been the daughter of this old couple. One of those wounded soldiers might have been their son. Maybe they witnessed that scene too. It broke my heart.

Although the old couple asked all about me, they never shared any information about themselves—where they had come from, how they got to the cave, what sort of work they did, or about their family and children.

I wondered who it was that brought the old man, whose limbs had been amputated, and the old lady, who was blind, there to that cave. They could not have possibly got there by themselves. I wanted to ask them several times, but could not bring myself to do so. The old man seemed wary of spies discovering the cave, and I felt, in my childish mind, that I ought not to ask too many questions, so I never even found out their names.

The Preciousness of Life

Seeing me deep in thought one day, the old man asked, "What's the matter, Tomiko? Are you lonely?"

"No, I'm not lonely," I replied.

"Really and truly?"

"Yes, really. Because I have you, Grandpa and Grandma." I looked at him intently and continued, "May I stay here always? I want to stay here with you and Grandma. I want to be with you when I die."

They both began to cry, even before I stopped speaking. When I saw that, I was filled with such emotion, too, that I couldn't go on. After a while, the old man spoke again.

"I'm grateful that you feel that way, Tomiko. That you want to die along with us. But Tomiko, you're still a child. You're strong. You mustn't speak of dying. You've got to keep your spirits up. Tomiko, the most precious thing in this world is human life. To be alive." Looking straight at me with his large eyes, he spoke slowly, taking great pains to make me understand.

"What will you and Grandma do?" I asked.

"We're fated to stay here."

They've made a pact to die here in the cave, I thought, and they are going to throw me out. I determined to tell them once more how I felt. This time I would try and make it very clear.

"Grandpa. Grandma. I want to stay here. Please let me die here with you. I haven't anyone else. I looked so hard for my sisters, but I didn't find them, so I'm sure they're dead. My brother Chokuyu died at Komesu. Two of my older brothers joined the army and went off to fight and haven't come back. My other brother went to the mainland and never returned. My oldest sister married and lived in Naha, but that's where the first bombs fell, and my father said the whole city burned and she must have died. And my next oldest sister got married and went to Saipan. So there's only me left. Please Grandpa, let me stay. Grandma, please ask Grandpa not to drive me away."

I had put my heart and soul into my plea.

The old lady could do nothing but sob.

"You needn't say another word, Tomiko," said the old man. "We understand."

So they understood, I thought, and looked up gratefully. But the old man's next words were not at all what I expected.

"Now listen to me carefully, Tomiko," he said. "I told you just now that human life is the most precious thing in this world. Now then, your life doesn't just belong to you. It belongs to your father and mother, too, who bore you, because even though they are dead, they go on living in you. You have their blood. Your blood is the same blood as your father's and mother's. So it's your duty to take care of it and live as long as you can. Do you understand what I've said so far?"

"Yes, sir," I replied.

"Right. You're a good girl, Tomiko. Well, as for us, you can see for yourself that we are not in very good shape and can't expect to live much longer. Naturally, we intend to live as long as we can but it won't be very long. You, however, know us well. If, when you're grown up, you remember this old man and this old woman and think about us sometimes, that's all we ask. Even if our bodies die, we will be able to live on in your heart. That will make us happy. Can you understand that?"

The old man gazed at me again with his big, kindly eyes. They were moist with tears. I did not say anything. I simply nodded. I knew if I tried to speak I would cry. But then, I decided to make just one more plea, and I looked up at the old man. But the look in his eyes had changed. His expression had become stern. It was not a bit like the "baby" I was in the habit of feeding. I realized then that however sad and painful, the day would inevitably come when I would have to leave this cave and part from this kindly couple.

From that time on, whenever they were not looking at me, I made a point of gazing at the faces of the old man and the old lady as much as I could. If I had had pencil and paper and had been able to draw, I would have made portraits of them. Failing that, I was obliged to use my eyes as a pencil, and my brain as a canvas, so I would not forget how they looked.

I tried not to think about the sadness of the inevitable parting, and made up diversions, such as plugging the cracks in the wall of the cave with my hands where water seeped through, and collecting pebbles and counting them. I also tried my best not to let our eyes meet.

Once, when the old man called me over to scratch him where he itched, and afterwards sat back and began to snore a little, the old lady, who was lying down, said in a tiny voice, "Don't you spoil him too much, Tomiko, because when you're gone, I'm the one who's going to have to do that!"

"Don't worry," I replied, pouting miserably, "I'm not going anywhere. I don't want to go away."

"No, no, Tomiko. Didn't Grandpa tell you just the other day how precious life is? He's absolutely right, you know. And besides that, Tomiko, even if you don't have any family, you can grow up and lead a fine life."

Not wanting to worry the old lady any more, for fear it would be bad for her health, I said, "Yes, Granny. I understand," and went back to playing with my pebbles.

When I had become thoroughly at home inside the cave, I made a discovery. I happened to be playing right at the back, where there was a crack in the floor at my feet. Water seeping through the walls of the cave drained into the crack, which I found ran along the floor of the cave like a gutter. It was connected with the hole which we used as a toilet. The water washed away our feces—a natural flush toilet! That was why, unlike the other caves that smelled of many people's urine and feces, this cave was a very pleasant place, with cool, fresh air always flowing through it.

I often recalled my father's words around this time. I would go to the back of the cave, where it would seem as if he was saying to me, "Tomiko, there is such a thing as fate. It's something you cannot reverse. You can't decide where or when you will die. If it's your fate to die, you'll die no matter where you happen to be." I was able to exist all alone on the pampas moor with the animals, after being separated from my sisters, because I had been quite prepared to die if that was my fate.

What a lot of animals I had seen there on the pampas moor! Goats, dogs, cats, and even a pig. I once ran smack into a goat, and as I was wondering whether it would run away in fright, it came towards me, bleating. When it was so close I could have put out my hand and touched its whiskers, there was an enormous bomb blast nearby that startled the goat so that it took off at tremendous speed through the pampas grass. The cats would disappear as soon as they saw me, but the dogs seemed quite tame and would come over, especially since I was a child. But I was wary of wild dogs, particularly after seeing three or four of them eating the flesh of a dead soldier. It was strange to think that even a mighty soldier could be vulnerable in that way. Whenever I walked through the pampas moor, I made a point of carrying a stick so I could drive animals away.

The pig was quite amusing. When we ran into each other, it put its head on one side as if to size up the situation, and satisfied that I meant it no harm, it simply turned its back on me and went off into the pampas.

There were the ants, of course, who led me to food, the rat who brought me the sweet potato, and Nini, the rabbit, who protected me from a direct hit by the incendiary bomb. I wondered where Nini had gone after his home was burned. I wondered if he was still alive and well somewhere.

Those were the sort of thoughts that passed through my mind as I played at the back of the cave. So long as I stayed out of sight I thought there might be a chance the old man would not tell me to leave.

FULFILLING MY DUTY

The Hurried Parting

Quite a few days had passed since I had come to the old couple's cave, and now I was living in a complex state of mind, torn between security and insecurity. One day, when I was playing at the back of the cave, I heard the old couple discussing something in whispers. I peeked around a bend in the cave to find out what they were talking about. The old lady was usually lying down a little apart from the old man, but now she was bending over in front of him, doing something. And what they were saying was this:

"Lets hurry and make a flag out of the front part of my loincloth. The American forces are right nearby."

"Yes, but how? We haven't got any scissors."

"Use your teeth. That's right. Your teeth. Tear it with your teeth."

"All right."

"Hurry! There's the loudspeaker again."

Just then I heard a funny-sounding voice outside the cave. It seemed to be speaking in Japanese, but somehow did not sound like my mother tongue. How strange. I wanted to hear what was being said, and ran past the old couple toward the entrance and listened. And this is what I heard:

"People of Okinawa, I am a Nisei. My father and mother are Okinawans. Please believe what I am telling you. Come out of there quickly. The American Army does not kill civilians. There is no time to lose. It is dangerous to remain in the caves. Bombs will be thrown into the caves very soon. Please come out quickly. People of Okinawa, the war is over."

We were being asked to surrender. It was a loudspeaker announcement. It was repeated over and over again, "People of Okinawa, I am a Nisei..."

"You see, we've got to hurry."

"Yes. Is this the right place?"

"That's it. Grip it with your teeth. That's right."

The old man sounded agitated. He said he was going

to make a flag, but I wondered what sort he meant, and went over to see what they were doing. The old lady seemed to have her head between the old man's legs and she was desperately trying to tear, with her worn, uneven teeth, the front apron-like portion of his loincloth. The old man tried to make it easier for her by twisting and pushing forward his limbless torso.

After some time had passed, when the funny voice on the loudspeaker outside the cave began its message again, the apron part of the loincloth had finally been torn off, and there was a single long white strip of cloth

"Now we must make it into a triangle," the old man said.

"A triangle?" said the old lady, feeling the cloth with her hands. "Shall I rip it from about here?"

"Yes. Tear it diagonally from there."

"To make a triangle. All right."

Once again the old lady began tearing the white cloth with her teeth that didn't mesh properly. Someone with good teeth could have done it much more easily, but not only were her teeth bad, but her fingers had become very weak, and she did not make much headway. But nevertheless, the old lady worked desperately.

"Keep it up! You've almost done it!" The old man had one eye on the entrance to the cave and one eye on the old lady's progress. Then he murmured to himself, "I hope it'll be in time."

"Have I made it a triangle?" asked the old lady, spreading out the piece of cloth for the old man to see.

"Yes. It's a triangle!" he said, nodding his head with

satisfaction. "You've done it! We're going to make it." Then he turned to me, looking much more serious than usual. "Tomiko, find something we can fasten this to. A long stick, or something. Hurry!"

I found a tree branch near the entrance of the cave and took it to the old lady, whereupon the old man said to her, "Tie it on securely so the knots won't come undone. Be sure and tie it securely. It mustn't come off under any circumstances. A precious life is at stake."

"Yes, I understand."

The old lady tried to tie the triangular piece of cloth onto the branch, but her eyesight was so bad and her fingers so weak that she could not tie the knots properly. I was unable to stand by any longer and offered to help, hoping I wasn't interfering, and the old lady and I together tied the piece of cloth that had been the old man's loincloth securely onto the branch.

"Is that all right? Do you think it will hold?" asked the old lady.

"Yes, that's fine," replied the old man. "That makes a splendid flag. Tomiko, try holding it."

I did as the old man said, and held the branch. As I did so, the old lady turned her sightless eyes in my direction and said, "Hurry Tomiko, off you go, holding it."

"What? Holding this? Me? I don't want to." Up to that very moment I had no idea the white flag was intended for me, and I was so surprised, I refused without thinking. And besides, even if they told me to take the flag and go, outside the cave there was that American out there speaking funny Japanese. If I went out holding this conspicuous white flag, I was sure I would be shot immediately.

"Tomiko, as long as you're holding that, you'll be quite safe," said the old man. "It's a symbol understood all over the world. You'll be absolutely safe."

"If it's absolutely safe, you and Grandpa come with me!" I said, catching hold of the old lady's hand. But the old man said, "We'll stay here. You'll manage all right alone, Tomiko. You must hurry and go." He looked at me very intently, his eyes opened wide.

"I want to stay with Grandpa," said the old lady. "We've been together for a long time, and I want to go on being with him. I don't want us to be separated." She gently pushed away my hand and moved back towards the wall and leaned her back against it, sitting right up close beside the old man.

I knew the old man was far too large to get through the tiny entrance to the cave, and the old lady too weak. But I thought there might be another entrance I did not know about through which they could escape without anyone seeing them. Otherwise, how could they possibly have got in? I thought there must be an entrance large enough for a grown up and looked around.

And then I thought of the night I saw an officer stab to death fifteen or sixteen badly wounded soldiers with his sword, one after the other. Even if there was another entrance through which the old couple managed to escape, what with the old man very badly wounded and the old lady's vision badly impaired, they would probably be killed on the spot if they were discovered by a

Japanese soldier. In that case, I reasoned, they would be better off here. I wondered what to do.

Just then the old man spoke: "You're a child, Tomiko, and the American troops would never shoot you. Americans do not lie."

"Then you and Grandma will be all right too. They said just now they would not kill civilians." I tried to persuade them once more to escape with me.

"Tomiko!" the old man barked, in a tone of voice I had not heard before. He sounded very stern indeed. And he threw me a look so sharp and grim that it quite took me aback.

I decided not to worry them by pleading any more. I stood up, holding the branch with the white flag tied to it like a staff.

"Grandpa and Grandma, thank you for everything." I said, with a little bow of my head.

"Good. So you're going," said the old man, vigorously nodding approval. "When you get outside, hold up that flag good and high so everyone can see it. And hold it straight. Got it? High and straight."

Those were the last words I heard him say.

When I had climbed up to the entrance of the cave, I turned around. The old man was sitting in the same spot in which he had been the day I first came to the cave, and he was staring at me in the same way. The old lady sat beside him, looking up toward me with her sightless eyes.

I raised my hand, and the old man nodded vigorously, over and over again. There seemed to be tears glistening in his eyes. I couldn't see them clearly, but I saw him wipe his eyes with his bandaged stump. The old lady seemed to be speaking to the old man, but I couldn't hear what she said.

After first passing the branch with the white flag fastened to it out through the cave entrance, I timidly put my head out. The brightness blinded me. I had not experienced direct sunlight since coming to the cave, and it hurt my eyes. I stayed like that for some time, with just my head outside, taking a look around me. There were no people in sight, and quite a long way off I could hear that voice speaking funny Japanese.

"Haven't you climbed out yet?" It was the old lady's voice from down below. Her voice sounded frail, but clear. It gave me the boost I needed to climb on out of the cave.

When I think, even now, about how the old man must have felt as he watched my little bottom disappear, and what was going through the old lady's mind when she said "Haven't you climbed out yet?" I am overcome with tears.

When I got out of the cave, I hurried off as far away from it as possible. I was afraid that if I hung about, someone might discover the opening to the cave and find the old couple.

When I thought I had covered enough distance from the cave to safely look back at it, I turned. I looked all around, but could see no sign even of the bracken that had indicated the entrance to the cave. There, finally I started to do as the old man had said and hold my tree branch, with the white flag tied to it, up high.

Quite soon, I came to a path with a low hill on one side and a cliff on the other. I suddenly realized that there were no sounds of gunfire and exploding shells, which I had heard incessantly as I had fled about the countryside.

The sun beating down on me made me perspire even when standing still. When we left our home in Shuri, the rainy season had just begun, and it had rained on and off the entire time I was wandering about, hiding, and the roads, and where the caves were, and even parts of the pampas moor had been so muddy it had been very hard to walk. But now it was high summer, and heat waves shimmered all about me. Even my triangular white flag, made from the old man's loincloth, seemed to be undulating in the summer heat. I could hear birds singing, and pleasant breezes caressed my cheeks. It was all so tranquil and serene it was hard to believe that this had been that same battlefield.

The picture of the old man and the old lady refused to leave me. And then I thought I heard my father's voice right nearby saying, "Tomiko, you must stick it out to the end," followed by my mother's voice saying,

"Tomiko, I'm right here with you." I looked around, but there was no one in sight.

Feeling a draught on my buttocks, I put my hand behind me and discovered that the back of my work pants were torn and were slipping down, leaving half my bottom bare. "Oh, dear! They'll fall down," I thought, and hitched them up with my left hand, supporting the branch with the white flag tied to it with my right shoulder as I started down a slope.

Presently, the path I was on was joined by another one coming from my right. Just as the old man had said, there was nothing to be afraid of, and beginning to feel lighthearted, I had quickened my pace, when I was suddenly aware of people on my right, and looking up, I saw two or three soldiers standing there whose faces did not look at all Japanese.

American soldiers! They were the first I had ever seen, and my heart missed a beat, with fright. I saw that one of them was holding something in front of his face with a round hole in it pointed directly at me. What could it be? It did not look at all like the rifles and machine-guns that Japanese soldiers carried. In fact it looked rather like the camera used in the Naha photographer's shop where we once had a picture taken of us as a family.

"Maybe it's a camera," I thought. "But on the other hand, maybe it's some weapon I don't know about. He's going to take a picture that will kill me."

When I was going from cave to cave, I heard people say American soldiers were very cruel and thought nothing

Hitching up workpants with one hand and holding the white flag with the other, the author begins to feel lighthearted.

Joining soldiers who are also walking to their surrender.

of killing people. They told me Americans cut women and children up into little pieces. These false rumors were spread by the Japanese Army to make the populace hate the Americans and think of them as ogres, so as to make people afraid to surrender. But I did not know that at the time, and innocently believed them.

"If that's a weapon," I thought, "this is the end. I'm going to be killed." Then I remembered my father's words, "If you come face to face with the enemy, don't let him see you cry. Die with a smile." So, right away, I looked straight at the round hole pointed at me, and smiled. At the same time, I let go my left hand that was holding up my pants and waved, and with my right hand, I gripped the white flag that had been resting on my shoulder, and held it high.

"Grandpa, Grandma, thank you for the white flag, but it didn't work. I'm going to be shot," I said to myself as I walked along, resigned to my fate, staring at the round hole from which I expected a bullet to come toward me any minute. But it never came. In a moment the round hole was right beside me and I heard a click.

As I passed the American soldier, I could not see his face because he was looking through the round hole, but his pink cheeks left a vivid impression in my mind. Although he was an enemy soldier, his plump cheeks gave him a kindly look.

Well, the old man was right after all, I thought. The white flag was an emblem of safety. I was still not entirely free from anxiety, but so far, there didn't seem to be anything hostile or scary about American soldiers.

I began to wonder if by any chance the old man and the old woman had had second thoughts about leaving the cave, or had perhaps been rescued by someone. I turned around and looked behind me, hoping I might see them, but I saw only two men in Japanese soldiers uniforms, joining the path I was on by another route. They looked far more animated than any Japanese soldiers I had seen heretofore and were actually smiling.

No matter how hard I looked, I could see no sign of the old man and the old lady in the distance behind the soldiers. "Oh, Grandpa, Grandma, why don't you come?" I called to them in my heart. "This is the white flag you made so desperately! This is your loincloth, Grandpa!"

I was climbing, now, and then the path began to go downhill. I broke into a slight run, still carrying my white flag. I heard no shots behind me. I seemed to hear the old man's voice saying, "It's all right now, Tomiko. It worked, didn't it?"

I finally came to a place where I could see the ocean. "I'm alive!" I wanted to shout at the top of my voice. "Grandpa, you were right!" But instead, I kept still and gazed at the sea, murmuring to myself, "Oh, Grandpa and Grandma, if only you could feel this wonderful sunshine and see the blue of the ocean!"

27-year-old John Hendrickson at the time he took the photo.

Feeling that the old man might be right after all—the white flag was an emblem of safety.

I decided to walk in the direction in which I saw some American soldiers. Although I didn't think I would be shot. I still felt the necessity to be careful, and thought it safer to be among the Americans, since they would not be apt to shoot at their own forces. On the way, I passed an American soldier with an arm band directing people where to go. Reassuring myself I would be all right because I had the white flag, I followed his directions.

Soon, I began to see more and more people. Their clothes were all in tatters, but their faces looked calm and relaxed compared with the people I had seen in the caves, and some were even smiling. And, curiously, the Japanese soldiers I saw were in uniform but did not have any rifles or ammunition pouches. How odd they looked!

I finally came down a slope to the rocky shore, where I waded through rock pools, which felt lovely after walking so long on the hot earth with my bare feet.

At the end of the rocky area I could see a sandy beach on my left, where a crowd of mostly women, children, and old folk were assembled. They had come out of caves after hearing the American Forces' loudspeaker announcement.

When I approached the throng, a Japanese man tried to take my white flag away from me. I dodged away from him.

"You won't need that any more. Give it to me," he said, taking it by force.

"Oh, but that's the flag Grandpa and Grandma put all their effort into making for me," I thought, gazing up ruefully at the white flag, which the man now held.

"What's your name and address?" said the man.

I stood to attention and in one breath recited my name, birthday and address in Shuri.

As the fighting became more intense, Father had taken me out into the garden every morning and instructed me, very strictly, "Tomiko, if you are asked your name and address, you're to stand at attention and give it." What he had taken such pains to teach me was standing me now in good stead.

"Shuri, you say." The man put his hand on my back and led me to one of the groups. Not understanding why I was there, I was looking up at the faces of the people in the group, when suddenly I heard my name.

"Tomiko! Tomiko!"

Before I had time to turn around I was being hugged with tremendous vigor. I looked up to see who it was, and saw it was my sister Yoshiko, whom I had imagined dead. My sister Hatsuko was with her.

"Tomiko! Tomiko, my darling!" Yoshiko took my face in both hands and shook it, and then burst into tears. Hatsuko stroked my hair and kept saying, "So you are alive! You are alive after all." She was crying, too.

But I did not cry. The reunion had been so unexpected, and besides that, my mind was still filled with thoughts of the old couple in the cave whom I had only just left behind. There were lots of people here much older than they, it seemed, and seeing them, I kept thinking, why, oh why couldn't Grandpa and Grandma have come with me, and be here too?

"Tomiko, are you injured anywhere? How are you?" asked Yoshiko, between sobs, turning me round and round.

"No, I'm not hurt anywhere. What about you?" I said.

"Why you little brat! You act as if nothing had happened at all," muttered Yoshiko. "But I suppose that's why you've managed to survive."

She put a finger in a hole by her knee in her work pants saying, "This was made by a bullet. Another fraction of an inch and it would have blown my leg off."

"Hatsuko, what happened to your arm?" I asked, noticing my other sister's left arm in a sling made of white cloth.

"I was hit by shrapnel from a bomb," she replied. "But it's not very serious."

"I guess brother Chokuyu was looking after us."

"Isn't it marvellous that the three of us are safe."

My two sisters held me between them and rejoiced together. It was just as if we were back home again at our house in Shuri.

So I was reunited with my sisters at last! For the first time I buried my face in Yoshiko's bosom. I was conscious of the warmth of one's own flesh and blood. And then the very warmth of her bosom made me once again think of the old man and the old lady who could not have been kinder to me or more loving had I been their very own grandchild.

I could not make up my mind whether to tell my

sisters about them or not. Letting go of Yoshiko, I sat down on the sand and did not speak for some time, just flipping sand with my finger.

Soon we heard a group of grownups, a little way off, screaming among themselves. We listened, and could hear them saying, "They're going to put us all in a big hole, pour gasoline on us, and set us on fire!"

How awful, I thought, just when we were sure we'd been saved, and we weren't even wounded. If they knew about the old couple they'd be sure to kill them right away, so I resolved not to tell anyone about them. Not even Yoshiko or Hatsuko.

I pictured us being thrown into a hole alive and set fire to, and became quite miserable. To think that now I would never be able to repay the kindness of my two handicapped friends in the cave!"

But the possibility of our own death, just when the three of us had been safely reunited after nearly forty-five days on the run in the midst of the battle, separated and without news of each other, somehow held no horror or terror for me. I had seen so many tragic deaths and cruel killings that I had ceased to have any reaction to death at all.

Eventually we found out that the story that we were all going to be burned alive was a rumor spread by some of the surrendered Japanese who had misconstrued American intentions.

At that point, those assembled on the beach were put into trucks to be driven to an internment center. As our truck moved off, I looked in the direction of the old couple's cave and silently spoke to them:

"Thank you, Grandpa and Grandma. You were right, Grandpa, the white flag really worked. Thanks to you, I am safe."

With each bounce over the potholes, I watched the hills behind us, where their cave was hidden, grow smaller and smaller.

"Grandpa, Grandma, sister Yoshiko and sister Hatsuko are safe too. We're all three together. And it's all because of you. It's all because you taught me that life is the most precious thing in the world, and that we mustn't treat it carelessly."

Tears started rolling down my cheeks.

"Tomiko, what's the matter?" Yoshiko saw me crying, and spoke.

"Oh, nothing," I said, shaking my head and managing a smile.

"That's all right, then," said Yoshiko, drawing my head to her.

I looked again for those hills where the cave was, but the truck had gone around a bend in the road, and the hills had disappeared from view. All I could see was the ocean. I closed my eyes and began again to converse silently with the old couple.

"Grandpa and Grandma, you gave me the courage to go on. Your cave was such a peaceful haven for me. I haven't told anybody about you. Not even my sisters. So please stay alive in your peaceful cave as long as you can. I promise you that I will never tell anyone where your cave is as long as I live."

Just then I heard Hatsuko's voice: "Tomiko must be awfully tired. She's fast asleep."

"I wonder where and how she lived," said Yoshiko. "A little child like this, all by herself."

"Yes, I was all alone at first," I replied silently. "But then I met an awfully kind old man and old lady."

The truck bounced over another pothole.

"Goodbye, Grandpa. Goodbye, Grandma."

According to American army records, it was the twenty-fifth of June 1945.

SEARCHING FOR
THE PHOTOGRAPHER

During the decades-long postwar American occupation of Okinawa I often came across illustrated books in English about the war, and would flick through the pages to see if I could find myself in any of them. I was aware that a photograph had been taken of me, although I still didn't know of the existence of John Hendrickson's photograph. One day in 1977, in a book I had picked up at random in a foreign bookshop in Okinawa City, then known as Koza, I saw it—a picture of a barefoot girl in ragged workpants carrying a three-cornered white flag. At last I had found my seven-year-old self again! I slammed the book shut and ran out of the shop, forgetting all about my shopping. I don't remember how I got back home, but the first thing I knew was that I was lying on my back on the tatami floor, my heart thumping. Then I tearfully began to relive those last moments in the cave.

For some time I told no one of my discovery—not even my husband. But several years later, something happened that brought the existence of the photograph to his attention, too. In 1983, a project was started called the "Foot of Film Fund," in which the citizens of Okinawa were each asked to donate the price of one foot of motion picture film. The goal was to buy the documentary film footage made by the United States Army about the war in Okinawa, so that it could serve as a permanent record to teach children about the misery of war. Footage was purchased little by little, and the following year a portion of it was shown on television. Who should suddenly appear on the screen but me with my white flag, facing the camera, smiling and waving.

"You know, the way that girl's holding that flag in her right hand and smiling, she looks just like you. *Is* it you?" asked my husband as he watched the program. I didn't say a word, but my husband noted that I hadn't said it *wasn't* me, and nodded significantly.

As a matter of fact, what I had just seen on television came as quite a surprise to me, too, for I suddenly realized I had been photographed not once but *twice*: by the photographer I had noticed, who had taken the still shot of me and whom I had been wanting to meet for so long, and by another cameraman filming a documentary movie for the official war record, who had taken me from a different angle. It had never occurred to me that there might have been another photographer.

I refrained from letting anyone but my husband know about my appearance in the film. I feared that revealing my identity would lead to a search for the exact location of the old couple's cave, which in turn would probably cause their remains to be collected and cremated for burial in a mass grave for those with no known family. I could not have endured that. I wanted them to sleep undisturbed, clasped forever in each other's arms, as they had wished. And besides, I thought, of what interest would the memories of a person who had been but a child, barely seven years old at the time, be to anybody?

But troubles began when all sorts of rumors appeared in the press about the girl with the white flag—stories that were not true, such as the conjecture that a soldier had made the flag. A book was even published, focusing on the photo of me with my white flag, but with a different girl's war ordeal! No one, of course, knew the wonderful story of the old couple's loving kindness. Shouldn't I come out and tell my story? I worried about what to do.

Then my husband said, "I think you ought to describe your experiences in the war. Tell it the way it happened. Record it for posterity. You're the only one who can."

So with my husband's encouragement, I contacted a teacher friend who helped me get the story published in a local newspaper under the headline: I WAS THE LITTLE GIRL WITH THE WHITE FLAG. After that, my desire to meet the photographer who took the picture, and thank him, grew stronger each day. But I knew I would have to go to America to search for him, and that seemed hardly possible. But miraculously, an opportunity presented itself in 1988 for a trip to New York. As a member of an Okinawan group, I was to take part in a Peace March in connection with the United Nations General Assembly on Arms Reduction!

On June 21, 1988, I took part in the peace march carrying a placard with an enlarged copy of the photograph of me holding the white flag pasted on it together with the words: SEARCHING FOR THIS PHOTOGRAPHER. I had made the placard in my hotel room the day before the march. Dressed as conspicuously as possible in a brightly-dyed Okinawan costume, with a crimson coral tree flower in my hair, I marched with others from the United Nations to Central Park, stepping jauntily in time to an Okinawan folksong played on a tape recorder.

Quite a few people spoke to me. "I don't know much about the war in Okinawa," said a woman with a child about five or six years old, "but judging by that photograph you must have had a terrible time. I do hope you find your photographer." A young man with a

Holding a placard in the New York Peace March.   *Kyodo Tsushin*

camera hanging from his shoulder said, "Photographers produce some unforgettable pictures. I'm sure the man who took that photograph remembers it. I hope for your sake that he's still alive." Another young man said, in a voice charged with emotion, "You don't usually think of love in connection with war, but the action of that man in taking your picture can't be considered in any other way."

I was quite sure then I would be able to find out about the photographer. But while my placard elicited countless suggestions about finding him, not one person said they knew him. Apparently the forty-three years that had passed since the battle for Okinawa was just too long a period. There was nothing for me to do but swallow my disappointment and go home to Okinawa.

But God did not forsake me. Or perhaps it was the old couple in the cave lending a heavenly hand of assistance. I did attract the attention of Fuji Television, which made a program about me and offered to help me in the search.

"We've been in touch," they said, "with Arthur Rothstein, who commanded the film unit in which the man who filmed you in his documentary served. He's informed us that the cameraman is dead, but that his widow is still living. What would you like us to do? Can you come to New York?"

"Yes!" I replied. "I'll come!" I could meet his widow! I could hardly contain myself.

I left Okinawa on the third of July, hardly able to control my excitement, and on the following day, at the

Japanese broadcasting company's New York office, I met Mr. and Mrs. Rothstein and Jane, the widow of the late Richard Bagley, the cameraman. It was truly a thrill.

Arrangements were made for the four of us to view the critical scene in the film. When it reached the point where I raised my hand, Mr. Rothstein suddenly said, "That's Hendrickson! He was the Combat Still Photographer," and pointed to a man in the corner holding a camera, with his face partly showing behind it.

Impulsively, I asked, "Is he alive? Where does he live?"

"In Texas," replied Mr. Rothstein.

"I'd like to go to Texas and meet him," I said, looking hopefully at Mr. Rothstein.

"John Hendrickson may not remember you. He's seventy years old."

"But as long as he's alive, I just feel I must go and thank him, if I can possibly get there," I persisted.

Mr. Rothstein then consulted with the man from the television company, who was in the room with us. After a while, the television man spoke.

"We'll take you there."

These kind people had granted my wish!

We arrived in Texas on the eighth of July. I was finally going to meet the photographer who had taken that picture! It was an hour by car from the airport to the Hendricksons' house, and I never knew an hour could be so long. I was jumpy, and could not settle down. Looking out of the car window, every time I saw a house standing in the middle of a lawn, I would think

"This must be it!" and get ready to rise from my seat. If someone was standing outside I would say, "Do you think that's Mr. Hendrickson?" until finally the man from the television company laughed, and said, "Mrs. Higa, we've only been going twenty minutes!"

At long last the car stopped in front of a house.

"Is this it? Is this where the Hendricksons live?" I asked excitedly as we walked toward the house. I could hardly contain myself and felt as if I were walking on air.

The door opened, and a tall, elderly man appeared. The moment I saw his face I exclaimed to myself, "It's those same cheeks all right!" His camera had hidden most of the face of the man who took my picture forty-three years before, but I had always remembered how bright and pink his cheeks were. He was older now but his cheeks looked the same.

"Forty-three years!" said Mr. Hendrickson, welcoming me with a warm handshake.

"Yes," I said, and couldn't think what to say next. I had thought of so many things I wanted to say when we met, but now I just stood there tongue-tied. Sensing my predicament, Mr. Hendrickson and his wife put their arms around me and led me into the living room, where we had a delicious tea, complete with Mrs. Hendrickson's lovely homemade jam, and reminisced about that time forty-three years ago. I felt as if I was that little girl all over again, and he was that 27-year-old photographer.

"Why did you wave to me?"

"Because my father told me that if I was about to be shot, to die smiling and waving."

"All I had was a camera, and you thought I had a gun! I'm so sorry. We couldn't tell the difference between your soldiers and your ordinary citizens. It was terrible. Here's the camera I scared you with."

He fetched his camera and held it up in front of him as if to "shoot" me. It was a large camera with a large flash attachment, but I couldn't see it very clearly because tears started to well up in my eyes.

"Don't cry, Tomiko. Forgive me for making you think of the war." His voice trembled with emotion, and so did his hands as he held the camera.

"Tomiko," said Mr. Hendrickson, "do you think you could smile at me and wave once more?"

Wiping away my tears, I faced the camera and raised my hand and smiled. The shutter clicked and there was

A wish comes true forty-three years later. He still had the same pink cheeks.

a flash. I felt as if a forty-three-year-old load had just been taken from my shoulders. But the Okinawa war was not over for me yet. I resolved then and there to write about my experiences in the hope that such suffering might never be repeated.

I should like to express my heartfelt gratitude to Mr. and Mrs. Hendrickson and Mr. Bagley's widow, Jane, for welcoming me so warmly when I was in America; Mr. and Mrs. Arthur Rothstein for informing me about Mr. Hendrickson; and to Joseph McCarthy, who helped me in so many ways. My deep thanks are also due to Mr. Takamaro Murakami and the other members of the Fuji Television News Center who rendered such assistance in locating my photographer, to Masao Eda of Kodansha, and to Dorothy Britton who translated my book into English.

Fatalities in the Battle of Okinawa

Japan		United States	
Imperial Army and auxiliary forces	94,136	Army	4,582
		Marine Corps	2,792
Civilians	94,000	Navy	4,907
Total 188,136		**Total 12,281**	

Source: Okinawa Prefectural Welfare Support Association and U.S. Army publication *Okinawa: The Last Battle*.

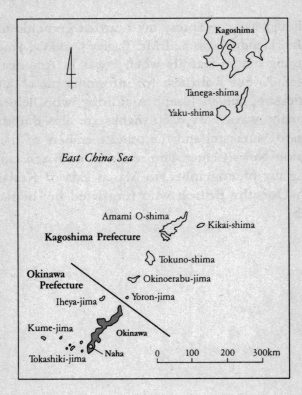